BFI Film Classics

The BFI Film Classics series introduces, interprets and celebrates landmarks of world cinema. Each volume offers an argument for the film's 'classic' status, together with discussion of its production and reception history, its place within a genre or national cinema, an account of its technical and aesthetic importance, and in many cases, the author's personal response to the film.

For a full list of titles in the series, please visit https://www.bloomsbury.com/uk/series/bfi-film-classics/

A poster designed for the overseas market

It Always Rains on Sunday

Lynda Nead

BFI

THE BRITISH FILM INSTITUTE
Bloomsbury Publishing Plc, 50 Bedford Square, London, WC1B 3DP, UK
Bloomsbury Publishing Inc, 1359 Broadway, New York, NY 10018, USA
Bloomsbury Publishing Ireland, 29 Earlsfort Terrace, Dublin 2, D02 AY28, Ireland

BLOOMSBURY is a trademark of Bloomsbury Publishing Plc

First published in Great Britain 2026 by Bloomsbury on behalf of the
British Film Institute, 21 Stephen Street, London, W1T 1LN
www.bfi.org.uk

The BFI is a cultural charity, a National Lottery distributor, and the UK's lead organisation for film and the moving image. We believe society needs stories. Film, television and the moving image bring them to life, helping us to connect and understand each other better. We share the stories of yesterday, search for the stories of today, and shape the stories of tomorrow.

Cover artwork: © Matthew Richardson
Series cover design: Louise Dugdale
Series text design: Ketchup/SE14
Images from *It Always Rains on Sunday* (Robert Hamer, 1947), Ealing Studios; 'The Haunted Mirror' (Robert Hamer), *Dead of Night* (1945), © Ealing Studios; *Pink String and Sealing Wax* (Robert Hamer, 1945), © Ealing Studios
Film stills courtesy BFI National Archive

A catalogue record for this book is available from the British Library.

Library of Congress Control Number: 2026000752

ISBN: PB: 978-1-8390-2694-2
ePDF: 978-1-8390-2696-6
ePUB: 978-1-8390-2695-9

Printed and bound in India

For product safety related questions contact productsafety@bloomsbury.com.

To find out more about our authors and books visit www.bloomsbury.com and sign up for our newsletters.

Contents

Acknowledgments

I should like to thank Sally Alexander, Sam Connor and Laura Mulvey with whom I first watched *It Always Rains on Sunday*, and Sally and Laura for ongoing conversations about this wonderful film. Barry Curtis, Katie Grant, Sarah Street and Melanie Williams have also shared my fascination and helped me develop my ideas and arguments. John Wyver has been a fantastic interlocutor not only through our series of discussions on post-war British film but also through regular visits to BFI archive screenings. Many friends and colleagues have contributed to my understanding of the film and the artistic culture of the post-war period: thanks to David Feldman for conversations about the Jewish East End; Frank Mort on the sexual morality of post-war London; and to Matt Cook and Richard Hornsey on masculinity and spivvery.

Thanks also to the staff at the BFI Reuben Library and the BFI National Archive for their enthusiastic help. And finally, my thanks to Rebecca Barden and Sophie Contento for their support throughout the publication process.

Introduction

> Thus a Sunday night in Stepney. Rain falling. Cinemas crowded. Public houses crowded.
>
> Youths playing on pin-table machines. Lovers in dark doorways. Trams and buses thundering and screaming down the main roads. Roads garish with neon and a hundred different sights, sounds and smells. And back of the main roads a wilderness of grey streets, little dwelling-houses, rows and rows and rows of them, intersected by gaunt blocks of tenements.
>
> Arthur La Bern, *It Always Rains on Sunday* (1945)

The first time I saw *It Always Rains on Sunday* (hereafter *It Always*) was in 2012 at the BFI in London; it was part of a season of films called 'Ealing: Light and Dark'. Although I went to many of the films screened during those months, the one that haunted me most was Robert Hamer's magnificent British noir. What was it that captured my imagination and made such a lasting impression?

Undoubtedly, it was the lead performance of Googie Withers and the outstanding supporting cast of British character actors, but it was something more than that, something almost visceral. After that screening, images and moments from the film kept returning: a young woman's crumpled dance frock; the sturdy arms, sensible dress and apron of a middle-aged housewife; a cluttered mantelpiece in a crowded kitchen; pictures of film stars pinned on a bedroom wall; faded wallpapers; wet pavements; the sound of boots on cobblestones; the cries of market traders; Yiddish slang; I could even conjure the smell of rain on heavy gabardine overcoats and vegetables cooking in a steamy kitchen. *It Always* captures entirely the 'hundred different sights, sounds and smells' described in the source novel by Arthur La Bern, but it intensifies and materialises them; they become expressive, poetic, historical and deeply atmospheric. As the film's press release pointed out, 'a prime consideration in the making of the film has been to try and capture the atmosphere in which these characters live'.[1]

Atmosphere is a complex and slippery concept. It feels like common sense to recognise the atmosphere of a film, or a piece of writing, a work of art, or, indeed, a place. It is, however, hard to pin down; attempt to define it and it seems to slip from your grasp. It is elusive, and rightly so. Yet it seems to me that the root of the power of *It Always* lies in its creation of atmosphere through photography, design, sound, direction, performances, lighting and screenplay. The film's distinctive quality is the way it makes use of its conditions of production to capture a specific historical atmosphere: the moment of Britain's faltering recovery from the effects of World War II. The year 1947, with its freezing winter, economic crises and shortages, permeates every frame of this film and its intensely dramatic evocation of the East End of London immediately after the war. Part domestic melodrama, part film noir, with a realism and authenticity that was admired by critics at the time, its release in November 1947 came at a moment when Britain had barely started on the process of reconstruction and remained a place of bombsites, rationing and Anderson shelters.

In reviving the notion of atmosphere, I am using it in a similar sense to the way that Raymond Williams employs 'structure of feeling' to describe those defining and distinctive characteristics of a culture that 'operate[s] in the most delicate and least tangible parts of our activity ... this structure of feeling is the culture of a period'.[2] It is something historically precise and significant but also deeply expressive. In 1948, Bill Brandt, who was regarded as one of the most 'contrasty' of the black-and-white photographers working in this period, described atmosphere as 'the spell that charge[s] the commonplace with beauty ... it is a combination of elements, perhaps most simply and yet most inadequately described in terms of lighting and viewpoint, which reveals the subject as familiar and yet strange'.[3]

This is as good an account of the atmospheric effects in *It Always* as any I have read. An ordinary street and ordinary people made strange and beautiful by the aesthetics of the film.

It is also a very English atmosphere, or, more precisely, a London and an East End atmosphere. Its mean streets are different from those of noir New York or LA. They are 'mean' in all senses, sinister, petty and deprived; they are also filled with longing, desire and resignation. And they are wet; the rain that falls throughout the Sunday on which the film takes place seeps into every scene, dripping down the backs of coats and off the brims of hats, obscuring the view from windows and leaving the night streets glossy and full of shadows. It is a damp and chilly world in which a family gathers in the kitchen because, unlike the rest of the house, it is heated by a range and where a broken pane of glass is given a makeshift repair with old blackout material. So, although atmosphere is a complicated basis for film analysis, I want to reclaim it and show just how palpable and moving it is in *It Always*. What follows is a summary of the film and its adaptation, and an outline of the key figures in its making. I also focus on the central factors that contribute to the atmosphere of the film and the moment of its making: its detailed composition of exteriors and interiors; its representation of women and female desire; and its depiction of men, the husbands, criminals and lovers of this tale of East End streets.

1 'The Secrets of a Street You Know'[4]

> NOTES TO ALL DEPARTMENTS: The indication (RAIN) in heading of scene means rain certainly required; (?RAIN) means rain may be required, depending on set-up ... In all non-rain sequences where exteriors are seen (even through windows and doors) some degree of post-rain wetness will probably be required.
>
> *It Always Rains on Sunday*, shooting script, 24 January 1947

An empty street of Victorian terraced houses, daybreak. Cut to the closed grille at the entrance to Whitechapel Underground station as a sheet of newspaper blows against the metal grating; a noticeboard tells us that it is Sunday 23 March. It begins to rain. The opening shots of *It Always* immediately establish the weather, the location, the time of day and the mood of the film. As the directions on the

shooting script clearly show, rain is an essential element in creating the atmosphere of the film and acts as a leitmotif that weaves together the diverse narrative strands.[5] *It Always* is the story, taken from a novel by Arthur La Bern, of one Sunday in the lives of a group of people living in the East End of London. Although the novel, which was published in 1945, is set immediately before the outbreak of war, the film brings the story up to date, to the immediate post-war years, in an East End that is still scarred with bombsites and homes that continue to keep blackout material in their Anderson shelters. The main characters are swiftly introduced in the opening minutes. In one of the terraced houses, a middle-aged man raises the blind of a window and watches as a young woman in a floor-length gown gets out of a car and enters the house. The car then drives past a coffee stall, where three small-time crooks in 'sharp' suits pull up their collars, thrust their hands in their pockets and walk out into the rain. Behind them, the stallholder reads a newspaper, which carries the headline 'Dartmoor Escape'. There is a cut to a railway embankment and a man, the escaped convict, running and sliding down the

Tommy, the convict, makes his escape in the rain

wet banks. The escape will trigger the sequence of events that will disrupt the apparently ordinary lives of these characters and bring physical and emotional violence to the quiet terraced street.

Inside the house at 26 Coronet Grove, the family at the centre of the story are waking up. Rose Sandigate (Googie Withers) is a former barmaid and is married to George (Edward Chapman), a dull but decent older man, who has two grown daughters, Vi (Susan Shaw) and Doris (Patricia Plunkett), from a previous marriage, and a younger son, Alfie (David Lines), with Rose. Rose lies in bed, knocks insistently on the bedroom wall and shouts at Doris to bring her a cup of tea, an apparently insignificant detail that reveals both Rose's general state of aggression and irritability, and the proximity and lack of privacy of the occupants in this home. In the bedroom the ordinary Sunday routine begins; Rose brushes her hair in the mirror and George reads his newspaper, telling his wife about the prison escape and the name of the prisoner, Tommy Swann (John McCallum). Rose is visibly startled, explaining that there was a customer with that name who frequented the local pub, The Two Compasses, when she used to work there. As Rose looks at her reflection in the mirror, a dissolve to an earlier time shows a younger Rose and her meeting with Tommy. She recalls their romantic courtship, his proposal of marriage and the appalling blow when Tommy was convicted of a violent robbery the night before their planned wedding. These memories are shattered by George asking what is for breakfast; an abrupt cut back to the bedroom and the present, as Rose blankly replies, 'haddock'.

Meanwhile, in the next-door bedroom, Vi is also waking and remembering a passionate evening. The sisters share a bed, and Doris notices that Vi is still wearing her gown. As Vi removes and hangs up the frock, her reflection in the wardrobe mirror dissolves to a dance the night before, where she catches the eye of Morry Hyams (Sydney Tafler), the married bandleader, goes for a drive with him and it is implied that they have sex. Although their own relationship is strained, both Rose and Vi are absorbed that morning by erotic memories and fantasies of a passionate life.

The family continue with their usual Sunday activities: Alfie asks for his pocket money; Doris washes up; and Vi goes to see Morry in his music shop in Petticoat Lane. Everything is as normal, almost banal, although Rose remains short-tempered and abrasive. She goes out to the Anderson shelter to fetch some old blackout material to mend a pane of glass in the back door and discovers that Tommy is hiding there and wants her help. Her manner with Tommy is different: for the first time Rose appears gentler and more caring. She agrees to smuggle him into the house as soon as the family are out and, from this point onwards, the normal Sunday routines are turned upside down. Familiarity becomes threatening and dangerous, and by the evening the tension for Rose will reach an unbearable crescendo. George takes his bath in front of the kitchen range, chatting amiably to his wife about his weekly darts match in the pub while she cooks the Sunday lunch. Eventually, the members of the family leave and Rose sneaks Tommy inside, where she dries his clothes, feeds him and takes him to her bedroom to sleep until

Tommy is physically out of place in the rooms in Coronet Grove

he is sufficiently recovered to leave. From this moment, there are two worlds in 26 Coronet Grove: upstairs, where Rose's former lover, Tommy, lies in her marital bed; and downstairs, where George and the family go about their normal Sunday business, oblivious to the drama that is unfolding in their home. These spaces also define two contrasting versions of Rose: upstairs, a woman of desire who belongs properly to the past; and downstairs, the frustrated housewife she has become.

Outside, the police are in Petticoat Lane market trying to track down Tommy and trace a 'gross' of roller-skates, stolen the night before in a failed robbery. There is also Slopey Collins (Michael Howard), a journalist, who is in Swann's old neighbourhood looking for a good story about the escape. Both will close in on Tommy and Rose as the day and night progress. Detective Sergeant Fothergill (Jack Warner), who is leading the investigation, questions the three crooks, Dicey (Alfie Bass), Freddie (John Carol) and Whitey (Jimmy Hanley). They are desperate to get some return on their pathetic haul from the robbery and go to visit their local fence, Caleb Neesley (John Salew), who covers up his illegal activities by posing as a pillar of the local church.

In Coronet Grove the strain on Rose is growing. She takes Tommy food and watches while he removes his wet clothing in the bedroom and puts on George's clothes. Tommy's presence in the house is uncanny; in each room he enters he seems out of place and physically intrusive. Even he admits, 'seems funny me sleeping in your old man's bed'. Tommy's younger and more muscular body inevitably recalls George's middle-aged one; Rose looks fondly and longingly at Tommy, and it is evident that she is still in love with him and desires him. He tells her that he needs money to make his escape to Cape Town and she goes to the back of a drawer and brings out the engagement ring that he gave her when they first met. While the ring clearly still holds significant meaning for Rose, it is equally obvious that Tommy has forgotten all about it, while idly suggesting that she should come and join him if he makes it to South Africa. This is the first of Tommy's betrayals of Rose that day which force her to acknowledge and accept the reality of her present life. A postcard to let her know that he is safe will be enough, she tells him.

After a strained family lunch, George has his Sunday nap in the front room. All seems peaceful until Vi, who is getting ready to meet Morry that evening, tries to retrieve her hand mirror from Rose's bedroom. The door has been locked and as Vi tries to force the handle, Rose rushes upstairs to prevent her from discovering Tommy. The hostility between the two women erupts in a shocking fight at the top of the stairs, during which blows and insults are exchanged and Vi's dress is torn. Rose surreptitiously unlocks the door and Vi, still furious with Rose, reclaims her mirror. Both are at wit's end; Vi leaves the house and phones Morry at home in front of his wife, Sadie (Betty Ann Davies), to tell him she is leaving Coronet Grove, and Rose sits alone at the kitchen table, tense with apprehension.

As night falls the mood in the East End becomes darker and more dangerous. Dicey, Freddie and Whitey drown their sorrows in The Two Compasses; Neesley has offered them a fraction of what they want for the roller-skates and Whitey is bitter and angry, threatening to 'do' the hypocritical fence. He leaves the pub and waits for him in the shadows of a railway arch, and when Neesley walks past, Whitey strikes him with a fatal blow and robs him. Things are also reaching crisis point for members of the Sandigate family. Vi has gone to meet Morry at the Palace dance hall and is confronted by Sadie, who tells Vi all his faults and then says she is leaving him. Morry runs after her, abandoning the disconsolate Vi. With only the sleeping Alfie in the house, Rose returns to Tommy and they make love; as he dresses to leave, Slopey Collins, acting on a tip-off from a barmaid at The Two Compasses, bangs on the front door. Desperate to make his escape, Tommy knocks Slopey out. As Rose pleads with Tommy to stay and tell the police that he forced her to hide him, he punches her to the floor and flees; the second and ultimate betrayal.

SALMON and
CUCUMBER
Shippam's

With Tommy gone, Rose gets to her feet, walks to the kitchen, locks the doors and turns on the gas oven.

Slopey informs the police about Tommy and they chase him through the dark, wet streets, finally cornering him in a railway marshalling yard, a strange, illegible space, filled with mist and steam, pools of light and deep shadows. Chased by Fothergill, Tommy dodges shunting engines and trucks and, as the police close in, he sees an approaching train and lies down on the track but is dragged off before he can kill himself.

As Tommy is arrested and taken away, a dissolve reveals Rose in a hospital bed, with George sitting by her side. He tells her that Tommy has been arrested and that she must get well because the family needs her. George's loyalty is both moving and imprisoning; the film dissolves to the locked grating at the Underground entrance and to the rain. As George walks back to Coronet Grove, the deserted East End streets were never more desolate.

* * *

The changes that were made to La Bern's source novel in the screenplay, written by Angus MacPhail, Henry Cornelius and Robert Hamer (who also directed the film), are fascinating and highly significant. Arthur La Bern was a Fleet Street reporter and war correspondent who turned to crime fiction and screenwriting. *It Always* was not his only book to be adapted into a film. His 1947 novel *Night Darkens the Street* was used for *Good-Time Girl* (1948) and, most notoriously, *Goodbye Piccadilly, Farewell Leicester Square* (1966) was the source for Hitchcock's *Frenzy* (1972), which La Bern disliked so much that he wrote to *The Times* dissociating himself from it. La Bern's life was tumultuous and had, at times, the drama of a feature film. According to his nephew, Peter Wickins, La Bern was 'a bit of a spiv';[6] he was a drinker and womaniser, who went from living the high life to bankruptcy and homelessness.

It Always Rains on Sunday was La Bern's first novel and is altogether darker, more violent and explicit than Hamer's film.

The brutality of the environment and its population is unrelenting and impacts all elements of the narrative. One of the most important changes in the film relates to Rose; played by Googie Withers she has a luminous beauty and although clearly intended to be middle-aged, she retains her star charisma. In the novel, Rose is

The luminous beauty of Googie Withers

described as large, pasty and wheezy, with a violent temper. Her physical size and unsympathetic nature are emphasised throughout and she is entirely devoid of glamour. It is also unclear whether she survives her suicide attempt and there is no reconciliation with George. The novel ends with George's return to the house in Coronet Grove and darkness.

The fight between Vi and Rose is even more violent in the book, with both displaying uncontrollable rage. Vi threatens Rose with a brass stair-rod and George hits both daughters and his wife, before beating Vi with the metal bar. It is an appalling episode that leaves the reader shocked at the cruelty and savagery of the Sandigate family. Although the changes in the film are clearly concerned with making the narrative more palatable to film censors and cinema audiences, they should not be seen simply as neutralising or sanitising La Bern's story. The film retains and enhances the novel's strong atmosphere of place and space and intensifies the dramatic tension of the central plot; the house in Coronet Grove is made even more compressed and confined. In La Bern's novel, Alfie sleeps in a bedroom upstairs, whereas in the film, the front room is also used as his bedroom, with the tense proximity of the two bedrooms on the first floor. The cramped landing between them is the highly focused stage for the fight between Vi and Rose.

The screenplay also heightens the fear that Tommy will be discovered in the house and the risks that Rose is taking in concealing him. In the novel, Rose is alone in the house when she becomes aware that Tommy is in the shelter; in the film, the rest of the family are in the kitchen when she goes out to get the blackout material, thus introducing the pressure of imminent disclosure that builds throughout the day. When Doris briefly returns home during the morning, La Bern has Tommy already secreted in the bedroom; whereas in the film he is still in the kitchen and must hide behind the door as Doris looks for a vase and collects her bag. Every episode involving a change of this kind progressively increases Rose's tension and Tommy's terror of discovery. It is, quite simply, a brilliant adaptation.

Perhaps the most outstanding addition in the film is the introduction of the final chase in the railway marshalling yard, which, for many critics, was the film's defining sequence. With the police closing in, Tommy clambers over a wall and drops into the marshalling yard. This final section of the film assumes a different character and quality from the previous claustrophobic domestic drama. With its backdrop of alternating pools of light and darkness, enhanced by the rain, mist and coal steam, it creates a dreamlike evocation of the industrial city, intensified by a cacophony of sounds, menacing soundtrack and shunting machines. Chased by the persistent Fothergill, Tommy runs across lustrous, rain-soaked tracks and jumps into coal trucks, but there can be no escape and he is led away by his captors, back to Dartmoor and the 'cat o' nine tails'. In terms of its shadowy aesthetic and dramatic treatment, this is the most 'noirish' scene in the film. Critics admired the cinematography, describing it as 'a brilliant bit of filmcraft' and 'as exciting as any Hollywood gangster melodrama'.[7] It has also contributed to the film's subsequent reputation as the cinematic heir to 1930s French poetic realism, such as Marcel Carné's *Le Quai des brumes* (1938) or Jean Renoir's *La Bête humaine* (1938).[8]

The rich chiaroscuro and shadowy imagery of the chase episode and its shift in register from the previous scenes may also have led, in part, to the creative attempts to define its genre. Described variously at the time and since as a 'documentary', a 'melodrama', a 'domestic drama', 'kitchen sink noir', 'East End noir' and a 'spiv film', it is perhaps obvious to say that the film is all of these things, and that its resistance to a single label is precisely because of its rich style and creative narrative. In the end, labels matter less here than affect; as Arthur Vesselo observed in *Sight and Sound* shortly after the film's release, 'It is a film with vitality, humour, and more than a gleam of atmospheric magic.'[9]

It Always represents the 'dark' side of Ealing Studios, the obverse of the 'light' comedies with which the studio is commonly associated.[10] While it has already been shown that these categories

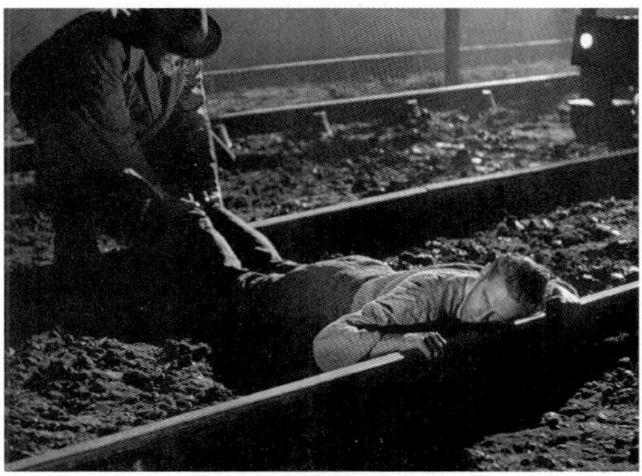

are scarcely watertight, it is undeniably the case that the film represents the underbelly of post-war Britain, with a dissatisfied population grabbing what it can, rather than a steadfast community cheerfully getting on with things. Occupying the site of a film studio built by Basil Dean in 1931, Ealing Studios Limited was set up as an autonomous production company in the late 1930s under the charge of Michael Balcon, who remained in control at Ealing for twenty years. In 1944, he negotiated a deal with Rank that offered financial support to Ealing while also allowing it to retain its artistic independence. Ealing is most distinctive for the ethos of the business, which was small, intimate and run almost as a family undertaking. It is also celebrated for having captured and defined the atmosphere of wartime and post-war Britain: when Balcon left the original site of the studios in 1955 he famously erected a plaque inscribed with the words 'Here during a quarter of a century many films were made projecting Britain and the British character.' Paramount to this endeavour was the continuity of senior staff at the studios. In the early 1940s, Balcon brought in a team of directors who worked on many of the key productions during the period and who, along with a small number of scriptwriters, cameramen and art directors, were put on permanent contracts and formed the creative core for Ealing projects.[11] The formation of a group of what Balcon described as 'like-minded people' effectively meant a white, male, middle-class and educated elite who created the distinctive style and ethos of Ealing film-making.

It Always combines the best of Ealing direction (Robert Hamer), cinematography (Douglas Slocombe), art direction (Duncan Sutherland), wardrobe design (Anthony Mendleson), artwork (James Boswell) and musical composition (Georges Auric); a team that both typifies and deviates from the homogenous circle created by Balcon. Robert Hamer was one of Balcon's regular directors and his career trajectory is in keeping with the Ealing system. He started out as a cutting room assistant for Gaumont-British studios, and during the war he joined the Government-funded

GPO Film Unit under Alberto Cavalcanti; when Cavalcanti moved to Ealing, Hamer went with him. At Ealing, Hamer was promoted to associate producer and was given his first directing opportunity on the 'The Haunted Mirror' episode in the brilliant portmanteau horror film *Dead of Night* (1945). Hamer's contribution is an uncanny tale of the resurfacing of a destructive and passionate past in the lives of a stylish modern couple, through the introduction into their new home of an old carved mirror found in a junk shop. Hamer plays on mirror reflections to evoke the spectral world, a trope that he uses again in creating the female memory world of *It Always*. It might also be argued that in the same way that the antique mirror in *Dead of Night* is the agent of repressed desire, so Tommy represents this threat to the house in Coronet Grove. The glamour of 'The Haunted Mirror' is produced in large part through the performance and appearance of Googie Withers, who plays the fashionable wife. Withers also

Googie Withers as Joan in Robert Hamer's 'The Haunted Mirror', *Dead of Night* (1945)

Googie Withers as Pearl in Robert Hamer's *Pink String and Sealing Wax* (1945)

had the main role in Hamer's next film for Ealing, *Pink String and Sealing Wax* (1945), in which she plays the beautiful, unfaithful and murderous wife of a pub landlord. Set in Brighton in 1880, several of the film's central themes, such as illicit female desire, unhappy marriage and suicide, reappear and are intensified in *It Always*. In 1949, Hamer directed his most well-known film, the dark comedy *Kind Hearts and Coronets*, which has come to exemplify the style and tone of post-war Ealing Studios.

Thus far, his biography fits comfortably, effortlessly, into the Ealing set-up and yet, in his memoirs, Michael Balcon wrote that Hamer was both 'one of the most remarkable of the young men I gathered around me' and was 'engaged on a process of

Robert Hamer

self-destruction'.[12] Born into a well-off Worcestershire family, Hamer was educated at public school and won a scholarship to Cambridge. A talented mathematician, his academic career ended when he was sent down for a year for what was most probably a homosexual relationship; he died an alcoholic at the age of fifty-two. Rather than a story of outstanding success, therefore, his life has been framed as one of wasted talent. Not unusually for this period, Hamer struggled to reconcile his homosexual identity and embarked on an unsuccessful marriage, as well as a long and destructive relationship with Pamela Wilcox (daughter of producer/director Herbert Wilcox). His addictive drinking made his studio work unpredictable, and following *Kind Hearts*, he had problems getting another project accepted at Ealing. Hamer was both an insider and an outsider in the studio; not simply one of the team, he was also an unruly and damaged maverick.

This may explain the distinctiveness of Hamer's film-making at Ealing, his intense exploration of buried and revenant desire and the powerful female presence in his films. Diane Morgan, a freelancer and the only woman screenwriter at Ealing at the time, declared, 'Ealing was a very male studio ... they didn't like actresses at all. So many of their films are male-dominated.' Morgan worked with Hamer on *Pink String*, observing, '[He] was just awfully good at directing women – no other Ealing films give such parts to women.'[13] Hamer's films for Ealing are exceptional; their fascination with thwarted sexual desire and their attention to female character make them especially significant within the studio's post-war output.

The powerful look and mood of *It Always* are also the creation of its director of photography, Douglas Slocombe. Slocombe had started his career as a photojournalist, moving on during the war to shooting newsreel and films for the Ministry of Information.[14] Like Hamer, he was persuaded by Cavalcanti to start working for Ealing; one of his first projects was on the framing story and Hamer's 'The Haunted Mirror' segment for *Dead of Night*. The chiaroscuro and heavy atmospheres in both create an increasing sense of claustrophobia and menace that Slocombe also brought to the photography of *Pink String* and *It Always*.[15] The high contrast in memorable scenes such as Rose's discovery of Tommy in the Anderson shelter, or when Whitey waits under the railway arch to rob Neesley, bear Slocombe's trademark style. It culminates, however, in the chase sequence in the marshalling yard, in which the realist elements of earlier scenes are utterly subordinated to the creation of a deeply expressive mood. The use of backlighting produces dramatic passages of illumination and shadow, and sharp reflections on metal rails and wet surfaces, a suitably climactic visual ending to Tommy's narrative.

The interiors are as remarkable as the shadowy, noir exteriors and are equally important in establishing the narrative and characters. Duncan Sutherland, the art director on *It Always*, was another of the long-standing staff at Ealing and was responsible for the overall visual style of the film. Each detail of the rooms in Coronet Grove, or Morry's music shop in Petticoat Lane, in Lou's arcade, or The Two Compasses pub, along with the wardrobe design, supervised by Ealing regular, Anthony Mendleson, perfectly embodies the nature of the place and its occupants. From beginning to end, *It Always* attends to the aesthetic value of details.

Ealing was unusual in this period in its use of contemporary British artists, such as James Boswell, John Minton and John Piper to design its publicity materials.[16] The opening credits are superimposed onto an illustration by the East End artist, Barnett Freedman, that immediately establishes the shadowy, urban setting; this mood is continued in the posters and marketing material designed by Boswell. The realism of *It Always* is thus undoubtedly part of and contributes to a wider debate within the visual arts in this period.

Poster design by James Boswell

Boswell, who worked on the publicity materials for *It Always*, was a founding member of the Artists' International Association, which had strong links to the Communist Party of Great Britain. His work belongs to a tradition of British realism that traces its roots to William Hogarth and eighteenth-century satirical prints, and draws on the graphic styles of Weimar artists such as Georg Grosz and Otto Dix. Boswell's artwork suits the brooding, rain-soaked world of *It Always*. In his design for the film's posters, the scene is contained within a brick arch, with two women walking arm in arm past a street corner lit by a large pub lamp; the edginess of the nighttime scene is emphasised by the women's uneasy expressions, looking to their left, at something just beyond the frame of the image. He was also responsible for the illustrations in the studio pressbooks, which were put together by the publicity department to promote the film and help cinemas in their marketing. A double-page spread depicting the teeming crowds in Petticoat Lane market is overlaid with smaller images, almost film frames, of the Sandigate kitchen, the spivs at

James Boswell's artwork for the press campaign book for *It Always* (Alamy)

the coffee stall and the home of Solly Hyams. The raw graphic style, which borders on caricature, captures both the hectic miscellany of the market and the individual lives played out on the street and in its homes. What sets Ealing apart from other film studios in this period is its rejection of traditional poster styles and its explicit and bold use of art for marketing. Although Rank evidently objected strongly to Boswell's allusive designs, the *Evening News* described them as 'the best poster and publicity decorations in the history of film advertising',[17] and Monja Danischewsky, Ealing's director of press and publicity, confirmed, 'the overall effect put a stamp of quality on the Ealing output as a whole'.[18]

2 Historical Atmosphere

It Always opened in November 1947, at the end of a hard year. It went into production in January 1947, cost just over £180,000 and was Ealing's most profitable film of that year.[19] A notoriously cold winter, which began in late 1946 and continued until March 1947, created appalling filming conditions for cast and crew. Heavy snow and blizzards during those months led to major transport disruption, and to energy and food shortages that exacerbated the already austere conditions created by ongoing rationing. Britain was in the grip of recession as the government struggled to restart the economy for peace rather than war. Faced with an economic crisis, the Labour government announced a package of stringent cuts and controls, and in 1946 bread rationing was introduced for the first time. Moreover, regulations had created the perfect conditions for a thriving black market and crime wave, with the emergence of the 'spiv' as the supplier of controlled goods to a public tired of restrictions and hungry for consumer goods. Indeed, to many it seemed that life was even harder in 1947 than it had been during the war.[20] This context not only set the conditions for the production of *It Always* but is also woven into the storyline. People and places were cold, a fact that determines the world of the Sandigates and how they spend that wet Sunday, preferring to be in the kitchen, heated by the range and cooking, than to go upstairs to the chilly bedrooms. Rain soaks the environment and its occupants, and it can come as no surprise that an evening trip to a warm cinema is suggested on two occasions during the film; a comfortable escape shared, of course, by its audiences.[21]

Rationing also impacted the film's production and is reflected in the plot. In a desperate attempt to get Doris out of the house, Rose tells her to take their coupons to the market and collect the cheese ration. Goods were equally restricted on the film set. John Collier's book *A Film in the Making*, which was published at the time of the film's release, sets out the story of how *It Always* was made and describes how the shortages affected the production.[22] For instance, in the fight on the landing, Rose tears Vi's dress and, in a rage, Vi rips it apart. In a world of clothes rationing and factory closures, the studio had only sufficient coupons to buy five copies of the dress, which had to be tracked down by the wardrobe supervisor.

The great fashion innovation of autumn 1947 was the Christian Dior 'New Look'; with its long, full skirt and nipped-in waist, it was a sartorial act of defiance against post-war austerity. Although Dior's dresses and suits were all over the pages of fashion magazines, they make no impact on the women of Coronet Grove. Other than a dressing gown in her first scenes and a hospital nightdress after her attempted suicide, Rose spends most of the film in a plain dark dress supplied, the credits show, by Horrockses, one of the most ubiquitous ready-to-wear labels of the 1940s and 1950s. Only in the flashback to her time with Tommy, does she wear lighter, brighter, patterned clothes and trimmed hats. Vi refers to the torn dress as her Sunday best, but it is also relatively plain. The costumes carefully, purposely, define these

women and their desires and aspirations; their clothes are modest, determined by restrictions and shortages, but they embody memory and fantasy. It is when Vi removes her dance gown in the morning and hangs it thoughtfully on the side of the wardrobe that she gazes in the mirror and recalls her night with Morry.

By the summer of 1947 a balance of payments deficit had deepened into a full-scale national crisis. With a massive drain of dollars from the country, the value of sterling fell, prompting the government to announce a new package of measures to reduce domestic consumption and to boost exports. Butter and meat rations were reduced further, potatoes were put on the ration for the first time and imports were once more restricted to curtail the flow of currency out of the country. Clement Attlee's Labour government introduced a package of tariffs and duties on overseas goods, and in August 1947, what became known as the Dalton Duty imposed a 75 per cent customs tax on all imported films.[23] As a Treasury official later explained to the House of Commons, '[if] we are cutting food, which is an essential to the life of the country, it is impossible to continue importing films and allowing a drain upon our dollar resources'; 'food before flicks' became the slogan of the supporters of Dalton's tax.[24]

With the majority of film imports coming from America, the Motion Picture Export Association of America (MPEAA) took immediate action. The following day it announced a halt in the supply of American films to British cinemas; although there were some already in the UK, in this period they accounted for around 80 per cent of British screen time and the stockpile would soon be exhausted. British exhibitors were most seriously impacted by the film duty, but it created turmoil throughout the entire industry. Although it was not a primary motive for the introduction of the tariff, the boycott presented British studios with an incredible opportunity to fill the imminent gaping holes in programming schedules. The question was whether those studios could increase their production levels sufficiently to compensate for the absence of American films. As quota levels for the exhibition of British films were raised, negotiations started between the British government and the MPEAA in the autumn of 1947, and an agreement to lift the duty and resume exporting films to Britain was reached in March 1948. The minute details of the talks and the resolution of the boycott are less important here than the fact that while production of *It Always* was in its final stages and at the time of its release, it found itself in the middle of a motion picture trade war. The trade journal *Kinematograph Weekly* summed up the situation, 'the fate of British production hangs in the balance';[25] and later, in 1955, the director general of the British Film Producers' Association admitted, '[it] nearly ruined the British industry'.[26] This is the industrial context of *It Always* – a film about shortages and compromises; about escape and opportunity; and above all, about uncertain recovery in a world of economic and social hardship.

There is an additional element that contributes to the film's historical atmosphere – the feeling and emotional quality of a British Sunday; everything in the narrative weaves around the particularity of that day of the week and its routines. Most people in post-war Britain would have agreed that the atmosphere of Sundays was tangible and different from the rest of the week and, even though it was 'the day of rest', there was nevertheless something generally gloomy about it. According to the panel of observers working on the Mass Observation (MO) study of national attitudes to and habits on Sundays, the day had become one of general aimlessness, often pleasant but mostly dull. The study, which was published in 1949, commented, 'the Sunday atmosphere is so pervasive that it affects even those to whom the religious and holiday values of the day are nothing'. Most effort was put into preparing and eating the Sunday dinner, for which the best rations were reserved and, not surprisingly, for many housewives it was plain hard work. One middle-aged London woman told an MO interviewer, 'I simply can't bear Sundays; it's a day which everyone regards as a rest day except for me ... my man sleeps in a chair; and I'm left with a load of dishes to wash up. I hate Sundays.'[27] No wonder it seemed to many married women as if it always rained on Sundays.

The framework of the Sunday routine – morning tea in bed with the *News of the World*, haddock for breakfast, preparation and consumption of dinner, a nap, an evening darts match in the pub – provides the scaffolding for the film and the ways in which its predictability becomes increasingly disordered and volatile. Rose's growing disconnection from the habits of everyday life is made more emphatic by the monotony of ordinary Sundays, which were regarded by many not only as a family day, but also as a national custom. As one Labour MP reminded the House of Commons, it was part of 'the British heritage ... one of our typically British institutions'.[28] Rose does not simply transgress personal values, therefore, she also transgresses national values.

Although many respondents to the MO Sunday survey complained that there was nowhere to go and nothing to do (cinemas did not open until late afternoon and, following a short midday opening, pubs remained closed until the evening), this is not the case for the inhabitants of 26 Coronet Grove. Unlike most places of trade and entertainment in this period, Petticoat Lane market was open on Sundays and was a hub of commercial activity. The MO report described the sights and sounds of the market – the banter of Jewish traders; ex-servicemen's bands; stalls selling nylons, herrings and puppies – and concluded, 'In Petticoat Lane there is little of the lethargy and aimlessness otherwise so common on Sundays.'[29]

Through a combination of location and studio work, *It Always* captures the buzz and diversity of the market in 1947 for audiences who had visited and those who had only read or heard about it. A studio tracking shot at the beginning of one of the Petticoat Lane scenes in which the camera is suspended by a crane and then moves down into the crowd, creates a vivid sense of the density and proximity of the milling throng. The sounds of the market are evoked as much as the sights, with the calls of the traders in English and Yiddish emphasising the diversity and vibrancy of the Jewish East End. The post-war market represented a transitional moment in the history of the customary Christian Sunday in Britain. Because most of the traders were Jewish, the Petticoat Lane market was exempt on religious grounds from legal restrictions. While some saw these concessions as an erosion of traditional social and moral values and

as symptomatic of the spread of the harmful influences of modern life, others viewed Sunday trading restrictions as inconsistent, unenforceable and increasingly out of step with the styles and wishes of British society.[30] *It Always* takes pleasure in the Sunday market; stripped of any religious significance but filled with cultural and ethnic references, it shows both sides of the post-war Sunday, the customary domestic routines and the attractions of public commercial life.

It Always is a paean to the British Sunday, and to the dark desires and crimes that lurk just below the surface of the rituals of ordinary post-war family life. In his book about the making of the film, Collier describes the rain 'as almost a character in itself';[31] it is there as a lowering presence throughout and, together with the temporal atmosphere of Sundays, is a crucial element in creating the film's style and mood. In his proposition that there was something incongruous about the idea of Britain and the art of cinema, François Truffaut famously claimed, 'the weather itself is anti-cinematic'.[32] I disagree; the weather is atmospheric, beautiful, and nowhere more so than in *It Always*.

3 The Genius of the Place

I think of *It Always* as a film about places and things, as much as it is about people. Some of my most intense visual memories are of the market and the pub, of Coronet Grove with its railway bridge and damaged church steeple, and the crowded rooms inside number 26. The concept of 'the genius of the place' derives from classical Roman religion and refers to the distinctive atmosphere or spirit of a location; it was revived in the eighteenth century to describe the effects of English landscape gardening and it might also be called upon to evoke a film's *mise en scène*. It certainly conveys the power of places and things in *It Always* and the brilliance with which these settings have been imagined and realised.

The original trailer features the studio recreation of Petticoat Lane with the words 'A picture hailed as the Symphony of London's East End', a claim that draws on the modernist cinematic tradition of city symphonies and promotes the film's artistic as well as its dramatic pedigree. The East End of London has always existed in the cultural imaginary as an idea, a myth, as much as an actual geographical place, with its significance boosted in the twentieth century by the Blitz, when it came to symbolise the resilience and fortitude of Londoners under bombardment. Jewish street trading had been a characteristic of Petticoat Lane since the mid-eighteenth century, but its identity as the centre of the British Jewish community came with the mass Jewish immigration from Eastern Europe at the end of the nineteenth century and the beginning of the twentieth century. By 1947, it remained a Jewish area, although the move out to residential areas to the north and west of London had already begun. The built environment of the East End continued to be dominated by Victorian housing and industry, pitted with bombsites, some cleared, others still strewn with rubble and abandoned cars. This is the grainy world of *It Always*; the urban landscape is broken, but the war is over and the process of clearing up has begun. The original setting of La Bern's novel in 1939 had to be altered to this post-war moment because the physical space was inescapable, it was intrinsic to the film's surroundings and constitutes its sense of place.

If the East End is both a material neighbourhood and a space of fantasy, then the West End in *It Always* is entirely a place of reverie. The narrative takes place in a clearly defined and bounded space; it is a film about and of the East End, and yet the West End is also evoked and becomes a crucial place of escape for the women, in particular. When Rose recalls her first meetings with Tommy, he offers to take her 'up West'; this is part of his glamour and desirability. She remembers one of those dates, when they visited a club and she won the jackpot playing the fruit-machine. For Rose, the West End is a place of romance and riches that could enable her escape from Whitechapel and The Two Compasses pub, but it is unreal and unreliable and she must return to the materiality of 26 Coronet Grove and George's haddock.

Doris, Rose's younger stepdaughter, is for the most part good-natured and compliant. She has a regular boyfriend, Ted (Nigel Stock), who is also pleasant but shows early signs of George's dullness. When she goes to meet him for a planned trip to Southend, she takes shelter from a rain shower in Lou Hyams's (John Slater) amusement arcade. Lou approaches her and makes conversation, offering her a job in a beauty parlour, 'a place up West, a real class joint'. When she sees Ted, she tells him about the job offer and he is immediately suspicious of Lou's motives; for Doris, however, it is her one moment of rebellion and aspiration. Like Rose, Doris's West End dream evaporates and she must remain an East End girl.

The East End created in *It Always* has a granularity and depth that is vivid, almost tangible, and is never reduced to background illustration. While places such as the market and its shops, the exterior of Coronet Grove and the rooms in number 26 are made coherent and legible by the production design, they can also quickly

become uncanny and hostile, through a shift from a realist register to a Gothic sense of fear or dread of discovery. Comfortable familiarity can switch to despair and betrayal.

Coronet Grove looks like any other East End terrace, with two rows of plain brick houses facing each other across a street with a few bushes and a single tree; its ordinariness is literally and metaphorically a front for the illicit desires within.[33] Every detail, each frame – a mantelpiece ornament, kitchen utensil, wallpaper or curtain – has a role in excess of any documentary function; as the strapline for the film's poster declared, 'The Secrets of a Street You Know'. Objects in *It Always* have an expressive verisimilitude that disclose the secrets within the familiar.

In his fascinating essay 'Architecture and Film', the film historian Peter Wollen makes the distinction between film sets that prioritise narrative and those that prioritise spectacle. The sets of spectacle, he argues, are static, architectural and dominating, whereas those of narrative are dynamic, subordinated to dramatic plot and almost unobtrusive. He lists 'masterpieces of cinema' (*Rome, Open*

City, 1945; *Brief Encounter*, 1945; and *The Third Man*, 1949) in which characters are strongly connected to particular surroundings:

> [these are] spaces which are lived in and used by the characters with whom they are associated. Often they are the settings for disaster and breakdown … the architecture of the sets is carefully designed both to dramatize and to be unobvious … *a reciprocal narrativization of décor and visualization of story-telling.*[34] (my emphasis)

To the sewers of *The Third Man* and the railway station buffet of *Brief Encounter* should be added the interiors of 26 Coronet Grove; an environment that is 'lived in and used by the characters' and which is also unobtrusive and dramatic: a stage for fury, sexual desire and suicide.

It is fitting, then, that throughout the film Rose is the only character who never leaves 26 Coronet Grove; she goes out to the Anderson shelter to collect the blackout material and she finally leaves in an ambulance after her suicide attempt, otherwise she remains confined, incarcerated, within her home. Rose's psychological experience of the house is different from that of the rest of the Sandigate family; each room becomes gradually charged with Tommy's presence and changes its meanings and associations. When Tommy is in a room, he often seems larger and more intrusive than the other characters; he is not at home there, he is a trespasser and we know that his physicality is both harmful and deeply attractive to Rose. Her mounting anxiety is expressed through the framing and lighting of these crowded interiors, the house appearing increasingly compressed and claustrophobic as discovery becomes inevitable.

The kitchen is the multi-functional space where family relationships are navigated and where desire is both extinguished (George) and aroused (Tommy). In his study of the making of the film, Collier observed, 'It is the focal point from which everything else of major importance springs.'[35] A memorable scene in the film shows

the Sandigate family in the kitchen on Sunday morning, with each figure embodying their role within the film, either through their pose or activity. While incidental narrative details such as George smoking his pipe, Doris clearing the plates and Vi varnishing her toenails are arresting, the fascination of the image is surely the kitchen itself with all its clutter and stuff. My eye is drawn to the kitchen sink, with its crooked draining board and racks of plates, the net curtain that sags in the middle and the birdcage at the window. It is cramped and modest, cheap in most respects, but it is looked after. Rose has been doing her domestic duty. It is also conspicuously out of date. At a time when the post-war modern kitchen was being promoted by government and commerce, the Sandigate kitchen is 'a hotch-potch of different styles and different times'.[36] In 1946, the *Daily Herald* 'Modern Homes' exhibition included three kitchen displays about which one female visitor observed, 'what a lovely lot of cupboards'. Cupboards are modern, streamlined, hygienic; in the Sandigate kitchen, however, things are on open shelves and hanging from hooks. This is an East End kitchen and, like the neighbourhood itself, still belongs to the Victorian past as much as it does to the post-war future.

There is a range and a gas stove in the kitchen and both play a crucial role in the plot. The range makes the room the warmest in the house and draws the family to its heat; it is where the clothes horse is placed and the washing is dried, providing a screen for George's bath. Rose boils the vegetables on the gas cooker, the steam adding to the warm, wet atmosphere of the room. The cooker also provides the means for Rose's suicide attempt; an unintended function of gas appliances that was to become a staple of modern drama and narrative.[37]

The mantelpiece is perhaps the most expressive element of this set, a frame for the film's 'structure of feeling'. Covered with a tasselled runner, it is a metonymy for the family's style and way of life.[38] With a clock at the centre, it bears a strange mix of functional and decorative objects, arranged with an eye to symmetry and order: a pipe rack and a container with pipe cleaners; a framed photograph;

a pair of scales; china ornaments. It is the sign of the family's history and habits and of what is at risk when Tommy Swann is allowed into the home. Above the mantelpiece a framed picture of a shipwreck transforms the image from film still to Victorian narrative painting, the set an artistic composition of symbolic elements that narrate the past and foretell the future.

I have gone into some detail in this account of the Sandigate kitchen because it is a testament to the care and attention that went into the production design and was a feature of the film that drew considerable critical interest. Most critics commented on the verisimilitude and authenticity of the settings, but they interpreted these differently. Some regarded the surface detail as characterising a prosaic or mechanical approach to fiction film, while others saw it as providing the social and psychological backbone to the story. The *Spectator* admired the accuracy of the setting but dismissed the film as a documentary rather than a drama; the *Graphic* described Hamer as 'a master of the realistic'; and the *Daily Worker* called it 'a carefully authentic tale'. More negatively, in his essay 'The Technique of Realism', published in *Sight and Sound* in 1948, film critic D. A. Yerrill accused Hamer of an excruciating attention to detail, with 'innumerable instances of extraneous material ... put into the film *simply because they exist in life*' (original emphasis).[39]

More reflective critics saw something greater than surface accuracy, however; something that the German sociologist and film theorist Siegfried Kracauer has referred to as 'the texture of everyday life'.[40] According to Dilys Powell in the *Sunday Times*,

> there is something more: an amused, a devoted attention to the tiny decorations of the everyday, to the chattering neighbour, the darts game and the black cat brushed with an exasperated gesture off the sofa-head. These trifles mark the difference between the studio set and the room lived in and an audience convinced of the realism of the scene it watches becomes submissive to the movement of the story.

This sounds a lot like Wollen's narrative sets, those that narrativise décor and visualise story-telling. She continues: 'The realism I mean is a different thing from documentary realism ... [concentrating] in a single moment what the lazy eye and mind take hours to see and comprehend.'[41] Powell has looked and thought carefully about the role of art design in *It Always* and about the significance of those interiors and the ways they animate and almost inhabit the characters. These 'tiny decorations of the everyday' are not just background, they are at the very heart of the film's 'atmospheric magic'.

One last review is worth quoting; the *Daily Chronicle* critic Paul Dehn applauded the performances of the principal characters but went on to suggest that what was most extraordinary about the film was the 'life' in the background details:

> This bedroom lives, because of its eiderdown; that front-door because of its post-war scaffolding; this wall, because it has a cat on it; that newspaper, because the house-number has been pencilled on its top right-hand corner ... So with the setting's every stick and stone.[42]

In the best criticism there is a give and take between the design, the narrative and the performances; for these critics, the *mise en scène* breathes life into every frame of the film. Hamer uncovers the poetry and beauty in everyday things and places; this is no simple transcription of the reality of working-class homes in the late 1940s and its recreation in the studio set; rather it is an evocation, an arrangement (in a musical sense) of those places and a concentration on the most significant details through the lens of a cinematic imagination. *It Always* is a film about the everyday familiarity of home and its undoing through the intrusion of buried desires. Within the house these states are not distinct but gradually merge and collapse through the genius of its production design and the language of objects. The film does not simply capture the reality of 1947, it gives it drama and poetry.

4 Blondes and Brunettes: The Women

Post-war Britain was as concerned with the recovery of family life as it was with the rebuilding of the nation's economy. War had transformed the lives of women and domestic life; marital relationships had been fractured and it was unclear how and whether they could be restored once men who had been serving in the armed forces returned home. This was not only a question of whether men could readapt, but also whether women would be satisfied with picking up on the lives they had led before the war. In the years immediately following 1945, politicians, sociologists and psychologists examined motherhood and childcare, divorce rates, and women and work. At the heart of many of these concerns was the unspoken question of female desire; and whether women would be content to reject the different social and sexual opportunities that they had been afforded during wartime in order to devote themselves to the family home and married life? What was the nature and future of marriage in post-war Britain?

Significantly, there are no references to the principal male characters in *It Always* having served in or been released from the armed forces. George is probably too old to have been registered for service; Tommy has been in prison; and the three crooks, Dicey, Freddie and Whitey, may have evaded call-up. Even Lou and Morry Hyams make no mention of wartime service and appear to be immersed in well-established habits and activities. Amid the crowd in Petticoat Lane, a couple of figures wear ex-army overcoats; otherwise the fighting seems to have passed all the male characters by.

Nevertheless, in many ways, *It Always* is a film about the war and its emotional aftermath. It is as though men have recently returned home, and the crisis in Coronet Grove is one created by the tension between duty, social expectations and women's individual desires. The choice faced by Rose between George and Tommy is an enactment of a more abstract dilemma facing women in the post-war years; will she be willing to reject romance, desire, aspiration and excitement in the interests of reconstruction and the restoration of home and nation?

It Always is one of a number of British films made in the second half of the 1940s about the role of women and the conflicting demands of restraint and indulgence.[43] This gives an added significance to the focus on the details of Coronet Grove and Rose's Sunday routine, and to the visual contrast between Rose's current life and her memories of the romance with Tommy. The repetition and ennui of her domestic life make the allure of Tommy and escape from her marriage stronger and more powerful and persuasive. Rose's dilemma is also suggested through the differences between Rose before and after her marriage to George, which are most

Rose's more glamorous look in the past

evident in the changes to her physical appearance and temperament. In La Bern's novel, the visual distinction is less pronounced; Rose in the present is a corpulent, asthmatic and abusive harridan, and she is described only briefly as having been a 'buxom, copper-headed barmaid'.[44] In the film, however, the changes are coded through a shift from a lighter, smarter appearance in which Rose displays a certain style of everyday female glamour, to a darker, more utilitarian look, with a plain dress and apron. As played by Googie Withers, however, Rose in both manifestations is a desiring and desirable woman. While it is clear this aspect of her present life has been suppressed, the brilliance of her performance lies in her recovery of sensual feeling and the revitalisation of her longing for Tommy.

A darker, plainer Rose in the present

Withers was born in 1917 in Karachi in present-day Pakistan, to an English father and a Dutch-French mother. Educated in England, she began her career as a dancer in musical comedy and was given her first film part in 1935. In her 1930s films, she is generally cast as a wisecracking, light-hearted blonde, continuing the type that she had played in earlier theatrical revues. In 1942, however, she played the role of a Dutch resistance worker in Michael Powell and Emeric Pressburger's *One of Our Aircraft is Missing*, which signalled her move to more serious and dramatic parts during the war years. From 1944, Withers made five films for Ealing Studios, three of which were directed by Robert Hamer; she later observed that she 'loved these meaty parts'.[45] It was during the shooting of the Ealing film *The Loves of Joanna Godden*, which was released in the summer of 1947, that she met and fell in love with John McCallum; they married in 1948, shortly after the general release of *It Always*.

Withers brings a distinctive physical and emotional presence to her film acting. Her characters are often working, if not working-class, women, who have a strength and assurance as well as a corporeality and sensuality that is very different from other styles of genteel English femininity in this period. In this way, Rose, as married to George, possesses an unadorned beauty and erotic potential, in marked contrast to her characterisation in the novel, and we are unsurprised that she has a deeply romantic and tragic past. The film emphasises the difference between Rose past and present by making Rose, the barmaid, a blonde and Rose, the wife and mother, a brunette. By introducing this visual distinction, the film taps into a much wider discourse concerning post-war British glamour, class, gender and respectability.

Blondeness in the 1940s and 1950s was grounded in popular images of affluence and consumption, but it was also a kind of aberration, unrestrained in its embrace of consumer culture and its self-regarding display of female sexuality.[46] Visually, it channels an awkward synthesis of Hollywood glamour and the everyday, gritty realities of post-war British life; glamour for working-class women in the 1940s could easily be interpreted as hard, unnatural and vulgar.

In 1948, the social researcher Pearl Jephcott published the findings of a study she had carried out on the lives and aspirations of young working-class women who had lived through the war and were now in their late teens. Noticing how much attention they paid to their hairstyles, she observed, 'Local hair-styles which dictate a combination of nine-pennyworth of peroxide, two-pennyworth of ammonia and a 25/- perm, may give a curiously brazen look to a mild little face below.'[47] This was the ambiguity of blonde; 'brazen', in this context, seems carefully chosen: bold, shameless and blatantly sexualised, it was not a look for respectable, modest women.

Blonde was a sign of social aspiration and personal dissatisfaction; a way of escaping post-war constraints and expectations. In the 1940s and 1950s, advertisers drew on the idea of Hollywood glamour to promote blonde hair dyes to women who longed for greater affluence and aspired to the look and romance of film stars. Advertising headlines and slogans suggested life would be fun and more thrilling with blonde hair, with one brand urging, 'Follow the stars and be a glamorous blonde'. As the British empire began to collapse in the years immediately after the end of the war, blonde femininity was a complex sign of racial whiteness and, at the same time, of sexuality and desirability, suggesting both absolute purity and utter artifice.

Advert for 'Golden Shadeine' blonde hair dye, *Photoplay* (March 1952), p. 50

Vi, the rebellious blonde sister; Doris, the steady brunette

The film's visual coding of the dress and appearance of Rose past and present is repeated in the figures of her stepdaughters, Vi and Doris. In the novel, both girls are blonde; in the film, Vi, the rebellious and spirited sister who is having an affair with Morry, is blonde, while Doris, the steady and acquiescent younger sister, has been made a brunette. Audiences in 1947 would immediately have understood the differences between the two women through this contemporary language of hair colour.

Blondeness also visually highlights the personal similarities between Rose and Vi and the subsequent tensions in their relationship. It is evident from the first scenes in the Sandigate household that Rose is a reluctant and inappropriate stepmother and that Vi does not consider her a mother figure, refusing to call her 'Mum'. Nevertheless, they have much in common and share a sense of frustration and longing and a desire to escape the banal routines of their everyday lives. Vi wants a career as a singer with a band and her attraction to Morry is, in part, because she believes he can arrange this for her. Vi is a dreamer, the bedroom she shares with Doris has

pictures of film stars pinned on the walls and many of her aspirations are focused on the way she looks. The discarded evening gown is an embodiment of her personal ambitions and seems out of place in her cramped bedroom in Coronet Grove, a crumpled reminder of her memories and her affair with Morry. Several of her scenes show Vi looking at herself in a mirror – in Morry's music shop, in her bedroom – and it is no coincidence that the incident that triggers the fight with Rose is the result of an attempt to retrieve her hand mirror from Rose's bedroom. The film suggests, and it was a widely accepted assumption in the period, that Vi's vanity, her dissatisfaction with her social position and her aspirations are linked; she is indifferent to Morry's wife and child, and her downfall is inevitable.

Rose and Vi create disturbance through their unruly desires; Rose threatens the stability of her own family and Vi splits up Morry's family (although this is clearly also a result of his own serial infidelities). In fact, all three Sandigate women feel trapped in the East End and have moments when they dream of something else, something better – Rose's lost happy ending with Tommy, Vi's success as a singer, Doris working in a West End beauty parlour. These episodes of fantasy or memory begin for Rose and Vi with mirrors and reflections, which are the gateways to their imaginations and desires. The most memorable of these scenes is when George reads the news of Tommy's escape to Rose in their bedroom. We see her reflection in the dressing table mirror as she combs her hair and there is a dissolve to Rose in the crowded bar of The Two Compasses. As she pours a drink from a hanging bottle, she catches sight of Tommy Swann in the pub mirror as he walks into the bar. He is young, sharply dressed and handsome, and as she turns back to the bar, and to the accompaniment of generically romantic music, they catch each other's eye and there is a long look of mutual interest. At this point we leave the world of reflections, although we remain firmly with Rose's memories. He buys her a drink and asks her out; a further dissolve reveals Tommy and Rose lying together in an idyllic pastoral landscape. This scene is different in all ways from any other

in the film. The two protagonists are totally unlike the selves that we see in the present in Coronet Grove and the style of this studio scene is in an entirely different register from the design of the rest of the film. This is a place of pure fantasy; with 'a symmetrically framed studio countryside', we are now in the realm of 'romantic fiction and film'.[48] Tommy gives Rose an engagement ring, promising they will marry when he gets back from a job. A further dissolve shows Rose prettily dressed and packing a suitcase for her wedding to Tommy; the pub landlord comes in and breaks the news that he has been arrested while carrying out a robbery the night before. There will be no marriage, at least not to Tommy. The soundtrack dissolves back to the bedroom in Coronet Grove before the fantasy image; George is asking what is for breakfast, it is raining and the pastoral fantasy evaporates.

This sequence perfectly captures Rose's personal and emotional situation. As the last lingering images, frames of memory, are punctured by George's banal question, the return to the rain and her life in Coronet Grove is painful to bear. We should be forgiven for thinking that Rose's memories are too good to be true; of course they are, these are thoughts that she has nurtured and treasured for over a decade. She is an unreliable witness and sees her past life through the lens of a different genre of fiction film, in which Tommy plays the romantic hero. In the present of Coronet Grove, Tommy is a desperate, violent, escaped criminal, who has forgotten about the ring and will abandon Rose to save himself. Even Rose is forced to admit that he is far from the figure she remembers when they first met. All three Sandigate women may dream, but their fantasies lead nowhere, and they are either rejected or must settle for the status quo. Better to be George or Alfie who seem to live wholly in the here and now and for whom haddock and a game of darts or a mouth organ are satisfying and attainable.

The cumulative strain of the day and of Tommy's presence in her marital home is conveyed by Withers's style of acting. There are no large dramatic gestures and only two outbursts of emotion:

when she fights with Vi and when she pleads unsuccessfully with Tommy to stay and support her. Instead, her performance is highly restrained and, as film historian Christine Geraghty writes, 'is based on a deliberately blank face, a rigid body and highly controlled use of gesture'. After the discovery of Tommy in the air-raid shelter, her growing strain is revealed through slight physical attitudes such as the stiffness and stillness of her back as she watches George replace the blackout material in the Anderson shelter, her eyes as she reads the newspaper with the family at the kitchen table, culminating in her hopeless resignation as she sits in the kitchen having been abandoned by Tommy and contemplates suicide. It is a powerful and moving performance that does not simply represent Rose's experience, but, as Geraghty suggests, gives 'a sense of what such a life might *feel* like' (my emphasis).[49]

5 Spivs and Husbands: The Men

In 1947, C. A. Lejeune, film critic for the *Observer*, dismissed *It Always* as a 'spiv' film, describing it as 'relentlessly gloomy' and deliberately ugly.[50] More recently, a number of film historians have placed it within a group of British films made in the years immediately after 1945 that address the criminal underworld, and which includes *Waterloo Road* (1945), *They Made Me a Fugitive* (1947), *Brighton Rock* (1948), *Good-Time Girl* and *Night and the City* (1950). Although each of the films in this 'spiv cycle' has a different take on the figure of the spiv and his environment, they share a noir aesthetic and an exploration of the social and moral impact of crime.[51] Made at the height of British cinema's fascination with the deviancy of the spiv, *It Always* sits at the heart of this category and makes the spiv the focus of its representation of masculinity.[52]

To appreciate what was at stake in releasing a spiv movie in this period, it is important to appreciate the spiv as a historical character and to consider why it mattered so much in Britain in the years around 1947. The spiv was a particularly British style of criminal; home-grown, urban and working class, he was different from the crooks and gangsters that populated American cinema at this time. While the spiv adopted elements of the dress, appearance and mannerisms of his American counterpart, like the British dyed blonde, these were given a decidedly vernacular spin, creating a character, at times a caricature, that was uniquely expressive of domestic concerns in the years after the war.

The conditions for the emergence of the spiv were created by austerity. With Britain at peace but bankrupt and the government tightening restrictions on bacon, bread, butter and potatoes, and goods of all types difficult to come by, the black market and illegal dealing were the inevitable illicit consequence of rationing and shortages. Enter the spiv as the middleman between the criminal underworld and the desperate consumers of wartime and post-war Britain; a wheeler-dealer who responded to the demands of the market, whose goal was evasion of all forms of legal restriction and who was indifferent to the morality of national survival and a rationally planned recovery. In the second half of the 1940s, the spiv emerged as a social type, a historical personality who blended fact and fiction and who embodied the conditions of life in Britain in the years after the end of the war. In terms of the national narrative of returning servicemen, spivs were the personification of deviant masculinity, evading conscription and indulging their own illegal desires as well as those of the black market and its customers. There was also a degree of ambivalence towards the spiv, however, particularly from those sections of the population who were disillusioned with the Labour government and by its programme of economic restraints. For them, the spiv was simply supplying a need that had been created by the shortages. In the years immediately after the war, however, the dominant image of the spiv was as the antithesis of the fathers and husbands who had gone to fight; an unruly character who resided in the bombsites and broken fabric of the post-war city and resisted official attempts to rebuild domestic and civic order. It was not until the end of the 1940s and early 1950s, when rationing was relaxed and the economy was beginning to recover, that the spiv could safely become a figure of humour, and whose appearance and mannerisms were the subject of indulgent caricature.[53]

In the period immediately after the end of the war, conditions were too bleak for this process of reinvention to take place, and the spiv was the focus of a moral panic about crime levels and social breakdown. These flashily dressed young men were seen as the products of wartime, when a lack of parental control and a general relaxation of discipline in the home had created a generation of boys who had grown up consuming American gangster films and thrillers.

The absence of father figures and the negative influence of popular culture were blamed for the rise of the spiv, who thrived in the war, despised honest work and was responsible for a criminal urban subculture.

In the year in which *It Always* was released, public fascination with the spiv was at its height. Between 1946 and 1947, official figures showed a surge in recorded crime and particularly robberies with violence. Newspaper journalists and columnists turned their attention to the spiv, who became the focal point for debates concerning rationing, illegal dealing and the crime wave.[54] As the balance of payments crisis worsened, the government increased its attacks on black marketeers, while Conservative critics blamed its economic policies for having produced both the illegal market and the surge in crime. Though the etymology of the word 'spiv' may not have been widely known, its connotations were clear; long articles in 1947 in newspapers such as *The Times*, the *Daily Telegraph* and the *Sunday People* defined the spiv as a social leech, unproductive and parasitic in economic, social and moral terms.

National newspapers carried out pseudo-anthropological studies; one of the earliest was by Bill Naughton in an article first published in 1945 by Charles Madge, a founder of Mass Observation, in his quarterly magazine *Pilot Papers*.[55] Taking the form of a conversation between the journalist and a London lorry driver, the piece was shortened and republished in the *News Chronicle* and set out the defining characteristics of post-war spivvery. The lorry driver points out to Naughton the tell-tale signs:

> he's a proper little Spiv ... See his spivy [sic] coat – the width of the lapels, the padded-out shoulders and how it is curled round his backside? See his shirt with the little tight collar? And the big knot in his tie? Notice how his hair is parted in the middle, and the wave at either side? ... See the style he held his cig. [sic]? And the way he spoke out the corner of his mouth? Did you hear him going on about 'bleeding red tape'? ... Spivs, they always talk like that.[56]

Alongside his distinctive fitted and tailored clothes, hairstyle and manner of speaking, the spiv even had a peculiar way of walking: 'You stiffen the shoulders, and lift them a drop. And walk knowing you are walking. Fancy little style it is, and there's no other walk just like it. It's a mixture of pub and pansy.' This is a fascinating new form of masculinity, tough but also trendy, Americanised while totally British, aggressively male and at the same time effeminate or homosexual. Little wonder the spiv became a fantasy figure in British popular culture.

The spiv has been perfectly described as 'mixing petty crime, gambling and the black market with proletarian dandyism, urban waywardness and celebrity posturing'.[57] Spivvery was a type of performance, a way of being, as much as it was an illegal criminal activity. It was a way of moving through the city and adhered to a specific urban terrain: pubs, dance halls, markets, street corners, boxing clubs and dog races. The spiv was commonly identified as a product of London, with its own West End (Soho) and East End variants.

Front cover of the *Spivs' Gazette* (1949)

By the summer of 1947, the spiv had become a mainstay of the daily and weekly press, and the anti-hero of British film and fiction; a vivid visual invention from the start, it was a simple move to caricature as the figure became more firmly entrenched in the cultural imagination. By 1948, a spoof magazine, the *Spivs' Gazette*, had appeared, satirising the spiv and his schemes. With contents including the Spivs' Union, a history of spivvery and a spiv glossary, one front page includes a cartoon of its president, Ivor Racket, with all the components of the physical type: padded shoulders; tightly fitted tailoring; large cigar; hat tilted at an angle; and a reference to long-established Jewish stereotyping that will be addressed later and in more detail in relation to *It Always*.

By 1947 the image of the spiv was an easily recognisable type in print and film. As an article in the *People*, published a few months before the release of *It Always*, states: 'He does no work. He pays no taxes. He produces nothing.'[58] This was the modern London spiv. There are a number of spiv characters in the film, but each is significantly different: there is the successful entrepreneur (Lou Hyams); the handsome wide-boy on the brink of destruction (Tommy); and then there are the three stooges, Dicey, Freddie and Whitey. Together they constitute the idle army, the social menace of 1947.

We first see the trio of small-time crooks in an early scene, sheltering from the rain at a Whitechapel coffee stall; in some ways they conform to the look and style of the spiv of popular culture, but they also significantly depart from the type. Dicey, Freddie and Whitey are desperate; they are not urban flâneurs, they do not stroll

confidently through their neighbourhood, they are hunched against the rain; hat rims drip and if their jackets are pulled tightly around their hips, it is because their hands are dug deep into their pockets for warmth. They are creased and damp and dangerous, and if there is any residue of glamour, it is plainly cheap and tarnished. The gang are about to carry out a robbery that will result in the theft of a gross of roller-skates, rather than the expected safe full of cash, and they will spend much of the rest of the film trying to get rid of this meagre haul. As they return to the coffee stall to establish their alibi, they discuss the failed heist, each blaming the other for the debacle.

Dicey, Freddie and Whitey inhabit the streets of the East End and The Two Compasses pub; at the bar their posturing and spivvy clothes are more visible, although there remains something worn and frayed about their jackets and coats and they can barely scrape the money together to buy themselves a round of drinks. They are a miserable and irritable group and when their fence, Neesley, offers them just five pounds for the roller-skates they become increasingly

volatile and menacing. Back in the pub, Whitey threatens to 'do' Neesley, and he leaves the others in order to carry out a mugging that will end in murder. There is nothing comical about these counterfeit spivs; they are down on their luck, petty criminals who are prepared to kill.

The first sight of Tommy Swann is as an escaped convict sliding down a railway embankment, hiding in doorways and making his way across bombsites to Coronet Grove. It is only through Rose's memories that we see him as the sharply dressed, self-confident spiv with whom she fell in love. Reflected in the pub mirror and seen at the bar, he is the perfect urban dandy, vain, arrogant and with an attitude that is immediately recognisable. In the shooting script Tommy is explicitly described as being 'flashily dressed'.

Tommy, the sharply dressed, self-confident spiv

The wardrobe department achieved this look by getting the suits specially made by tailors who were told 'to make them a little "larger than life"', exaggerating the defining features of spiv tailoring and creating an extreme spiv look.[59] This is Tommy as he enters Rose's life; a romantic figure of sorts, but dangerous and essentially an illusion.

In the present, Tommy is cold, wet and ragged, desperate for a bite to eat and some warmth. While he retains a compelling physical presence in the house, even Rose observes that he is now a shadow of his former swaggering self. Tommy's physicality is constantly emphasised in *It Always*; from the moment Rose tells him to remove his wet clothes and put on some of George's dry ones, his body is an object of fascination. In the bedroom, before getting into bed, he

Tommy, the escaped convict

takes off his jacket and Rose sees the scars on his back left by prison whippings; she turns away, unable to look at them. Later, when Rose returns to the bedroom, tells Tommy that she has never stopped thinking of him and, in effect, still loves him, the strength of her desire is shown when they embrace and she places her arms underneath his jacket, feeling his bare skin and caressing the injuries on his back. This is the most erotic scene between them, and one that marks the continuity of Rose's love and her enduring frustration with George.

The female counterpart of the spiv was the good-time girl. In 1947, the journalist Ethel Mannin wrote a series of articles titled 'The Trouble with Young People', in which she described the hard, American glamour of the young women who hang around spivs, 'with bleached or brassy hair, greasy scarlet mouths done up from corner to corner'.[60] Blaming Hollywood films for both spivs and good-time girls, she sees them as shoddy copies of American prototypes, with no morals or social conscience. Rose is never properly a good-time girl; although she is blonde and glamorous when she meets Tommy, she is in love with him and believes he will marry her; spivs, however, are not husbands. This is one of the defining characteristics of spivvery; as Bill Naughton's informant tells him, 'A spiv never marries, unless he has to; and not often then, for he'd sooner pay. It sort of kills him: he gets that something about him – what a wife does to a bloke – that never fits a spiv.'[61] The spiv is a loner who will only live off a woman, and it seems doubtful that Tommy would ever have married Rose. A minor character in *It Always* confirms this apprehension; as Detective Sergeant Fothergill carries out his inquiries in Petticoat Lane, he speaks to a woman who is another of Tommy's former lovers. Still angry at being jilted by him, she vengefully directs the police to Rose.

Throughout the film the spivs, the police and the press shadow and close in on each other, exerting growing pressure and tension on the normal patterns of everyday life in Coronet Grove. Both within and beyond the film there is a reciprocal relationship between crime and the tabloid press in this period; they trace the same urban topography – the market, the pub and the streets – and involve men who live outside the conventions and expectations of domestic life. Their values and ambitions are not necessarily antithetical; a police colleague tells Fothergill he would not mind a pair of stolen roller-skates for his kid, and the reporter, Slopey Collins, questions the same local characters as the detectives and is the first to track down Tommy in Coronet Grove. Crime, journalism and the law are equal parts of the East End landscape and are represented by the group of non-husbands who populate the film.

Rose's husband George is one of the few figures of firm and steadfast masculinity in *It Always*. For all the emotional uncertainty and inconstancy of the spiv, George is the husband who stands by his woman and is predictable and reliable; when Tommy observes that George is much older than Rose, she explains, 'he's alright;

Edward Chapman

he's decent to me'. Edward Chapman, who plays George, is a familiar figure in post-war British film and television; he played both dramatic and comic roles, often as a patriarchal, officious character, or as a straight man to Norman Wisdom. His face and figure are slightly round and formless and he always seems a sensible type, with his hair neatly combed away from his face, wide side parting, and often sporting a thick moustache and round National Health glasses. In many of his films, including *It Always*, his posture is upright, with chin jutting forward, pipe in hand or thumbs stuck in waistcoat pockets. This physical bearing is exceedingly important; it establishes both the hitherto respectability of the house in Coronet Grove and the nature and extent of Rose's betrayal with Tommy.

It Always shows us the Sunday routine through the eyes of George as well as Rose. Although we focus on the mounting tension and danger confronting Rose, we also see George trying to carry on as usual while appearing out of his depth and bewildered by the emotional outbursts and capricious behaviour of the women in his family. He seems most at ease playing the mouth organ with his son, or with his male companions in the pub who appreciate his amiability and his skills with the arrows. It is apparent that George appreciates the slow tempo and habits of Sundays; he looks comfortable sitting up in bed with his tea and newspaper, enjoys seeing Rose preparing lunch, and looks forward to his afternoon nap and his regular visit to the pub. There are also signs that Rose has been a good enough wife; as George leaves for the pub, he searches in vain for his pipe cleaners and Rose quickly presents them to him from a drawer in the kitchen table, meticulously performing her role of caring wife and homemaker. This makes Rose's growing resistance and remoteness even more painful to witness. As the 1949 MO report revealed, Sunday evening was the one time in the week when men went to the pub with their wives; this has evidently been the normal routine for George and Rose. Not on this Sunday, however. As much as George tries to stick to his regular arrangements, Rose resists them, resulting in small but painful rejections. When he is finally dressed and ready for the pub,

George is comfortable with his Sunday activities – playing the mouth organ with his son and darts with his pub friends

George asks his wife whether she will come to watch him in the darts competition. Rose, who is desperate to be on her own in the house with Tommy, excuses herself because she has a headache. George's subsequent sympathy and offer to bring her back a bottle of beer are both irritating and moving. On the one hand, they demonstrate his tolerance and goodwill, on the other they confirm a certain disinterest and vapidity. The subtlety of Chapman's performance is to convey both qualities; George is a nuanced characterisation.

In all ways, George proves himself to be the antithesis of Tommy. In Rose's present life, George is normal, decent, conventional, dull and unsexy, whereas Tommy is exceptional, disorderly, rebellious and deeply seductive. The difference in their sexuality is made most manifest by direct visual and physical contrasts. We see George's body

as he vigorously washes himself in a bathtub in front of the range in the kitchen, screened by the towels drying on the clothes horse; a run-of-the-mill Sunday activity, it is certainly not an erotic display as he scrubs his legs and under his arms. Tommy, whose body is exposed when he removes his wet clothes, is younger, bigger and more muscular than George. In his study of the film, Collier describes John McCallum as 'a very masculine actor ... with outstanding physique'.[62] Tommy's masculinity is out of place in Coronet Grove, a domestic space moulded by the unassuming corporeality of the husband, rather than the spiv.

The contrast between George and Tommy is emphasised most forcefully in the scenes in which Tommy wears George's clothes or occupies his bed. In the morning, George sits in bed with the newspaper, his pyjama jacket buttoned up to the neck and the collar curling up on one side. The eiderdown also keeps him warm, and the whole ensemble conveys practicality and familiarity without intimacy. When Tommy is in the bed, his chest is naked under his

Filming Rose and Tommy in the bedroom at Coronet Grove

George in the marital bed; Tommy transforms the marital bed into a place of desire

Rose and George avoid looking directly at each other

jacket, and his behaviour with Rose sexualises the previously asexual space. Rose sits on the side of the bed and then embraces him; she is a willing partner, and the eiderdown is now more of an obstacle to their desire than a necessary comfort. When Rose first meets Tommy and later, when he is in the bedroom, they gaze directly and longingly at each other. Rose rarely looks straight at George, however; she has her back to him in the bedroom and when he has his bath, and the open newspaper often obstructs one of their faces. They are inscrutable to each other; dissimulation has become habitual and will reach a crisis point on this Sunday.

In the characters of George and Tommy, the husband and the spiv are two extremes of masculinity; there is a different kind of husband, however, in the figure of Morry Hyams, the band leader and saxophonist. In the earliest scene in which Vi meets Morry at the Saturday night dance, it is not made known that he is married and just how bad a husband he is. After the dance, Morry takes Vi for a drive in his car, he admires her singing and suggests that he can help start her career; they kiss and it is implied that they may have had sex (a point made explicit in the novel). The next morning, Vi is clearly as much enamoured with the idea of getting a job as a singer with a band as she is in love with Morry. The morning also reveals that Morry is married to the long-suffering Sadie and that they have a young child. Sadie is tired of Morry's affairs and is now angry and vengeful; she discovers that Morry has lied to her about the time the dance ended on Saturday and that he stayed out late for other predictable reasons.

Morry spends Sundays in his music shop in Petticoat Lane, standing at the counter in front of a poster with his photograph advertising 'Morry Hyams, the man with sax appeal'. Morry represents a different hybrid form of masculinity, a combination of spiv and husband. He dresses in flashy tailoring, with spivvy wide shoulders and lapels and sartorial flourishes such as pocket handkerchiefs; he is a vain man and a coward. He wants his affairs with non-Jewish young women (who are referred to by Sadie as 'shiksas' – a disparaging Yiddish word), but he also wants his wife and family home. By the end of the day, his wife will have left him

Morry
HYAMS
MAN with SAX APPEAL

and his affair with Vi will have ended. Vi refuses to play by the rules of Morry's extra-marital affairs and twice encroaches on his domestic life. She first arrives unannounced at the shop, and while Morry is clearly shaken by her unexpected appearance, he softens, and they are soon kissing in a listening booth, where they are seen by Vi's brother, Alfie. She is also in the shop when Sadie arrives; a meeting that proves to be the final straw for the exasperated wife. Later in the day, Morry is shown theatrically performing his roles as father and husband, playing energetically with his son while his wife sits nearby. The phone rings and Morry answers; it is Vi telling him that she has argued with her parents and is leaving home and needs his help. Sadie overhears a woman's voice and Morry's awkward responses, and there can be no going back on her revenge. At the Palais that evening, Vi turns up as arranged … and so does Sadie. She joins Vi at her table and proceeds to give her advice on how to look after her overindulged husband and the best way to wash lipstick off his shirts; as Morry rushes over to rescue the situation, Sadie makes the perfect exit.

6 A Symphony of the Jewish East End

One of the most intriguing exchanges in the film takes place in the music shop between Morry and his brother, Lou Hyams. To understand its full significance, it is necessary to take a detour through the post-war Jewish East End and the contexts of Anglo-Jewish identity in 1947. Lou is the most successful of the criminal characters in *It Always*. The East End is his turf; he knows everyone and is shown running his arcade, fixing fights and trying to offload the stolen roller-skates. He also has money; he buys Dicey, Freddie and Whitey a round of drinks in the pub and they clearly admire and respect him. In the afternoon he goes to visit his father, Solly (Meier Tzelniker), and his sister, Bessie (Jane Hylton); while there he tells Solly that he should move out of the East End and join the Jewish community in Stamford Hill, in north London. In addition, he hears about the financial hardships facing the youth club that Bessie runs; she refuses his offer of money but later in the day he turns up at the club and donates £50 to pay for its new gymnasium. With his cigars and gambling, Solly describes Lou as 'a bad one'; his money is nefarious, but his motives are ambiguous. Does he want to offer Doris Sandigate a job up West, does he want to seduce her, or both? Does he genuinely want to help the youth club, or is he trying to impress and outmanoeuvre Bessie?

Lou is a complex character, and his visit to Morry in the music shop is a brief and awkward one. I remember the scene mostly because of the gloves Lou is wearing when he comes into the shop, smoking a cigar, and leans on the counter to talk to his brother. They are striking fur gauntlets and look like a large animal's paws and wrists, rather than a pair of gloves. This style of glove was worn in the period, and they are clearly intended, like his cigars, to show Lou's wealth and ostentation; nevertheless, they also convey a strong

DECCA

sense of Lou as animalistic or not quite human and are in excess of any narrative function. Perhaps it is a coincidence that when Morry plays with his son, he is on all fours with a lion skin rug draped over his back and head. There are no other references of this kind in the film, and it remains puzzling why the two Jewish brothers are styled in this way.

Any discomfort created by these allusions can only be heightened by historical context. As shown on the front cover of the *Spivs' Gazette*, there was a strong association of Jewish traders and black marketeering that drew on well-established Jewish stereotypes. During the war this connection had been reinforced by consistent press reports of Jewish involvement in prosecutions for illegal trading of controlled goods, and a popular myth had been ingrained in British culture that Jews had gained from the war but had not contributed to the war effort. Comments at the highest levels of the British establishment repeated this allegation. Ernest Bevin, Foreign Secretary in the post-war Labour government, complained about the Jews of Europe 'pushing to the front of the queue', and during the crisis of 1947 suggested that Jewish black-market traders were hoarding fuel.[63] Although Bevin's personal attitude to the Jewish question has been debated by historians, the point here is that when Lou and Morry appeared in *It Always*, it was within a context in which the loyalty of British Jews was being questioned and where old and new stereotypes were in play.

If, as the trailer claims, *It Always* is a 'symphony of London's East End', then, inescapably, it is also a symphony of London's Jewish East End. Jewish settlement in the area from overseas began in the seventeenth century, and by the middle of the eighteenth century the Sunday market in Petticoat Lane was already associated with Jewish street trading. By far the greatest growth in the area, however, was at the turn of the twentieth century with mass Jewish immigration from Eastern Europe. The concentration of these German- and Yiddish-speaking groups made the Jewish community far more visible and culturally distinct. Increasingly, Jews were linked within mainstream British society with poverty and crime, leading to the passing of the Aliens Act in 1905, which restricted their immigration into the United Kingdom. By the beginning of World War II, middle-class Jews had begun to move out of the East End, preferring the more suburban areas in the north and east of London; those who remained were mostly older and working-class groups. Lou's uncle, we learn, has already left, and Lou tells his father that he should also abandon the noise and dirt of the East End and join the community in Stamford Hill.

The Jewish characters in *It Always* constitute a parallel narrative to that of the Sandigates and Tommy Swann; the two are connected but also have a distinct culture and set of concerns. The Jewish characters are a heterogeneous group, representing different generations and occupations, varying degrees of religious observance, and a mix of class, gender, wealth and social status. They are shown at home, in the streets, at work and volunteering at a youth club;

Lou visits his father and sister, a contrast of generations in the Jewish East End

they relate closely to each other (speaking in Yiddish, eating pickled herring or drinking kosher wine), but also interact easily with the other non-Jewish sections of the East End population. The different types of Jewish identity are most clearly shown in the contrast between Lou and Morry and their father, Solly. Solly is played by Meier Tzelniker, a Yiddish actor who immigrated to London from Russia in the 1920s and who ran the Yiddish National Theatre Company. When Lou visits him, Solly is wearing a skull cap and has a bottle of kosher wine on the table. A gentle man, he seems perplexed by the modern world of his scheming son and most at home in his East End community. There is a sensitivity in *It Always* to the generational changes in immigrant identity and to the nature of assimilation and its impact on community.

Antisemitism was as much a part of the Jewish East End as the Jewish community itself. From the beginning of the twentieth century, far right, nationalist groups had chosen the East End for the focus of their campaign against Jewish immigration, reaching a peak in the second half of the 1930s with the emergence of Oswald Mosley and his British Union of Fascists (BUF). In 1936, the BUF organised a march through the East End of their supporters in their blackshirt uniform. The demonstration was opposed by a coalition of trade unions, socialist groups and Jewish organisations, and the ensuing 'Battle of Cable Street' has since gone down in East End history as one of the most notable episodes of mass resistance to fascism and racism. In spite of the strength and unity of the anti-fascist response, however, the BUF increased the number of its supporters, and antisemitism continued throughout the war, resurfacing even more forcefully after 1945.

In the Michael Balcon correspondence at the BFI National Archive, there is a letter that problematises the depiction of the Jewish community in *It Always*.[64] It is addressed to Balcon, c/o Ealing Studios, and is from the Reverend Louis Shaposnick, minister of the Great Garden Street Synagogue, one of the largest and most important synagogues in the East End in the first half of the twentieth century. The letter is dated 3 December 1947, just days after the film opened, and is worth quoting in full:

Dear Sir

Your film now showing at the Odeon Leicester Square W. has caused deep concern among many film-goers of the Jewish faith, because of the ridicule and dangerous anti-semitic propaganda that it disseminates. That you, a member of the Jewish faith should be associated with so perverted a film is strange and inconceivable.

Sitting in the cinema one could over-hear the base remarks made against Jews in general by non-Jews as the film depicted Mr. Hyams as gay philanderer, black-marketeer and mean racket-driver. Your film is a fine contribution to the advancement of pro-fascist ideas.

I should indeed be glad to have your version, maybe I and many of my co-religionists are wrong? I wonder!

Yours faithfully

L Shaposnick

Balcon replied on 5 December, explaining that as a 'proud Jew' he rejected Shaposnick's accusation and pointing out that the associate producer and co-author of the screenplay, Henry Cornelius, was also Jewish. Balcon further defended himself by citing those critics who had described the representation of Jews as 'well balanced'; for example, the *Daily Express* had referred to the accusations of antisemitism but had defended the film against this complaint.[65]

Shaposnick's letter makes uncomfortable reading, and Balcon must have viewed it as a most unwelcome response to his latest film. As suggested earlier, the Jewish characters in *It Always* are a diverse group, representing the complexity of Jewish culture in the East End at that time; the accusations of antisemitism therefore seem to me to be quite unjustified. There were, however, very specific circumstances that might have made the Jewish community particularly sensitive to questions of representation and prejudice and that might explain Shaposnick's stance.

In the summer of 1947, newsreels and the pages of national newspapers were filled with the details of one story, the violent murder of two British army sergeants by Zionist paramilitaries Irgun Zvai Leumi (IZL) in Mandatory Palestine. The men had been kidnapped in retaliation for the execution of three IZL fighters and were later hanged, their bodies left in a eucalyptus grove and the ground around them booby-trapped with an explosive device.[66] British public opinion was outraged by the atrocity and, fuelled by existing beliefs that Jews were responsible for the black market, the incident provoked a violent backlash against Jewish communities and properties in several British cities, including Manchester, Liverpool, Glasgow and the East End of London. The antisemitic riots of August 1947 were the most widespread that Britain had ever seen; news images of smashed Jewish shop windows were a traumatic reminder of the terrors of Nazi Germany and exacerbated existing pressures on Jewish/British relations. On 29 November 1947, at exactly the time that newspapers carried their first reviews of *It Always*, Britain abstained from the vote of the General Assembly of

DAILY EXPRESS

No. 14,708 FRIDAY AUGUST 1 1947 FOUNDED BY LORD BEAVERBROOK Weather: Warm One Penny

PALESTINE THUGS THREATEN MORE KIDNAPPINGS

ATTLEE MAY TELL OF CUTS IN BREAD AND BUTTER

HOLIDAYS ABROAD BANNED FOR BRITISH CHILDREN

HANGED BRITONS: Picture that will shock the world

Food from abroad is cut

BUTTER RATION MAY BE HALVED

Food from our land is wasted

Cabbages fed to sheep

Food in the Argentine is rotting

Senor Miranda burns the oil

£100,000,000 lost in ten minutes

6,000 holiday trips stopped

By paralysis

CONTINENTAL holidays for 6,000 British children were suspended last night.

ABBEY WEDDING FOR THE PRINCESS

On November 20

PRINCESS ELIZABETH and Lieutenant Philip Mountbatten will be married at Westminster Abbey at 11.30 a.m. on Thursday, November 20, it was announced from Buckingham Palace last night.

THE CEREMONY—

—AND THE GUESTS

4 a.m. LATEST

'INVADERS ARE ON THE WAY'

Tel: London CEntral 8000 Manchester CEntral 2112

30s. policy

Precautions

Prisoners escape

300 in a week

Shots in Tel Aviv: 5 Jews die

From PETER DUFFIELD: Jerusalem, Thursday

FIVE Jews were killed and several wounded tonight in a clash in the all-Jewish city of Tel Aviv, 12 hours after the finding of two sergeants hanged by Irgun thugs in a sweet eucalyptus grove.

The police, in an official statement, blamed "men described as troops and police."

The statement said: "It is alleged that an armoured car fired upon a bus, killing one man and wounding a woman."

'JEWS MUST ACT'

STAY-PUT JEWS FOR CYPRUS?

2 DAYS TO GO

999 at midnight —woman held

He was named to Shinwell

Cripps asks: Free Empire trade

Tripper killed

IN A GROVE OF EUCALYPTUS…

WANTED: For murder

MENACHEM BEIGIN

Jailed man fights for his round

£200 profit

Teacher, aged 7, trapped in river

Chinese held

Dust-coat men raid store

Baby, 1½lb.

36,000 divorced

BACK PAGE, COL. ONE

'Hanged Britons: Picture that will shock the world', *Daily Express*, 1 August 1947 (Alamy) the United Nations in favour of the partition of Mandatory Palestine, the withdrawal of all British troops and the creation of independent Jewish and Arab states. This is the background to Shaposnick's letter, which now sits in a file among many containing Balcon's Ealing correspondence and which, in December 1947, carried so much emotion and fear. Balcon understood that as well as anyone and defended himself quickly and unequivocally.

Epilogue

There cannot have been a more exceptional and volatile moment for *It Always Rains on Sunday* to land in British cinemas. With its powerful narrative of post-war marriage and infidelity, spivs and violent crime, loyalty and desire, the film spoke to some of the key concerns of the first years after the war. Some of these circumstances, such as austerity and reconstruction, it might have anticipated; others, such as the climactic violence and partition of Mandatory Palestine, it could not have known. As I worked on this book and the inventory of events in 1947 grew, the richness of the grainy black-and-white photography, the detail of the settings, the complexity of the characters, also gained significance. From those first weeks of severe winter when the film was being shot, through to the balance of payments crisis and the introduction of the Dalton tax; the privations of austerity and rationing, and the response of the black market; the moral panic concerning spivs and violent crime; the fears of social breakdown and divorce; and the rise in antisemitism and the riots of August; it was a year in which the cost of war and its impact on peace became most clear and hit hardest.

This is not simply a matter of putting a film in its historical context, rather it is a question of understanding the ways in which the moment when it was conceived, designed and made are woven into every scene and frame. The range of sources drawn upon here amplify the rich textures of the film and enhance its 'atmospheric magic'. It enables us to imagine how audiences might have viewed this East End symphony, how they may have felt about Sundays and reacted to the peril facing the Sandigate household. Perhaps it was raining on the day they saw *It Always*, and the cinema offered a warmer setting than the streets and their houses; did they notice the eiderdown and the fur gauntlets, the sexual frisson between Googie Withers and John McCallum? To this extent *It Always* is an outstanding expression of Raymond Williams's concept of a 'structure of feeling'. The film captures both the familiar and emergent social and cultural forms of the age, giving them a poetry and dramatic intensity that is memorable and moving.

There is, of course, one more event that made 1947 a very special year. On 20 November, Princess Elizabeth and Philip Mountbatten married at Westminster Abbey. The bride was dressed in a gorgeous gown designed by Norman Hartnell (using clothing ration coupons to pay for the dress), and the ceremony was broadcast by BBC Radio to 200 million people around the world. After the service, a wedding breakfast was held at Buckingham Palace and the royal couple went onto the balcony and waved to the huge crowds assembled below and along the Mall. It was, everyone agreed, a fairytale wedding. If Elizabeth and Philip represent the idealised version of marriage in 1947, then Rose and George represent its imperfections. Perhaps it was good enough before Tommy Swann resurfaced and shattered the everyday lives of Coronet Grove; although Rose's barely buried anger and resentment suggest that her experience has been less than satisfactory and that is has left her emotionally and sexually unhappy and bored.

Each time I watch *It Always* and Tommy idly suggests to Rose that she should come and join him in South Africa, I run an alternative fantasy ending. Instead of betrayal, capture and attempted suicide, Tommy gets away and sends a postcard to Rose telling her where to meet him. Rose repacks her leather suitcase, and a final scene shows them reconciled and embracing in a new world, far from the East End of London. I cannot be the only viewer who has wished that Rose would also have her fairytale ending. But what a terrible film it would have made. Tommy must, necessarily, let Rose down again; he is, after all, already a fantasy figure, and Rose's torment is that George must forgive her and life in the Sandigate household will carry on as before. Another Sunday, rain, the newspaper, tea in bed and haddock for breakfast.

Notes

1 *It Always Rains on Sunday*, Pressbook, small, PBS 33754, Pressbooks Collection, BFI National Archive.
2 Raymond Williams, *The Long Revolution* (London: Chatto & Windus, 1961), p. 48.
3 Bill Brandt, *Camera in London* (London and New York: Focal Press, 1948), p. 11.
4 This phrase was used as the strapline for the film's trailer and marketing materials.
5 *It Always Rains on Sunday*, Shooting script, S126, Special Collections, BFI National Archive.
6 On La Bern, see Cathi Unsworth's introduction to Arthur La Bern, *It Always Rains on Sunday* (London: London Books, 2014), pp. 7–19, 12.
7 *Evening News*, 27 November 1947; *Evening Standard*, 28 November 1947.
8 A comparison made by Iain Sinclair, 'Tales from Mean Streets', *Guardian*, 24 April 2009; and Elliott Stein, who described *It Always* as 'the most French-styled British film ever made', 'Once More With Ealing', *Village Voice*, 30 May 1995.
9 Arthur Vesselo, 'Films of the Quarter', *Sight and Sound* (Winter 1947–8), p. 137.
10 The history of Ealing Studios has been thoroughly researched, most notably in Charles Barr, *Ealing Studios: A Movie Book*, 3rd edn (Berkeley, Los Angeles and London: University of California Press, 1998), on which the following summary draws, and more recently Mark Duguid, Lee Freeman, Keith M. Johnston and Melanie Williams (eds), *Ealing Revisited* (London: BFI/ Palgrave, 2012).
11 On the organisation and economics of Ealing, see John Ellis, 'Made in Ealing', *Screen* vol. 16, no. 1 (Spring 1975), pp. 78–127.
12 Michael Balcon, *Michael Balcon Presents … A Lifetime of Films* (London: Hutchinson, 1969), pp. 162–3. On Hamer, see James Howard, *More Than Coronets: Directed by Robert Hamer* (Consett: Ink Inc., 2015).
13 As quoted in Sue Harper, *Women in British Cinema: Mad, Bad and Dangerous to Know* (London and New York: Continuum, 2000), p. 57, and Howard, *More Than Coronets*, p. 91.
14 On Slocombe's career, see Duncan Petrie, *The British Cinematographer* (London: BFI, 1996), pp. 138–41.
15 Slocombe also worked on Joseph Losey's *The Servant* (1963), which, in common with *It Always*, focuses and intensifies the psychological drama in a contained domestic space.
16 The director of press and publicity until 1948 was Monja Danischewsky, a former art student from Russia; thereafter the role was taken on by John Woods, a painter, designer and art critic. See Nathalie Morris, 'Selling Ealing', in Duguid, et al., *Ealing Revisited*, pp. 91–100. On Ealing posters, see David Wilson (ed.), *Projecting Britain: Ealing Studios Film Posters* (London: BFI, 1982).
17 *Evening News*, 27 November 1947.
18 Monja Danischewsky, *White Russian, Red Face* (London: Gollancz, 1966), p. 142.
19 The film went on general release at the beginning of 1948.
20 For an excellent social history of the period, see David Kynaston, *Austerity Britain 1945–48: A World to Build* (London: Bloomsbury, 2007).

21 Doris's boyfriend, Ted, suggests a trip to the cinema; George also attempts to coax Rose into a better mood by offering to take her to see a film.
22 John W. Collier, *A Film in the Making (featuring 'It Always Rains on Sunday')* (London: World Film Publications Ltd, 1947).
23 The Dalton Duty was named after Hugh Dalton, the Chancellor of the Exchequer. See Ian Jarvie, 'British Trade Policy Versus Hollywood, 1947–1948: "food before flicks"?', *Historical Journal of Film, Radio and Television* vol. 6, no. 1 (1986), pp. 19–41.
24 Financial Secretary to the Treasury, Hansard, House of Commons, 2 July 1947, col. 1448 ff. As cited in Jarvie, 'British Trade Policy Versus Hollywood', p. 29.
25 'British Studio Section Supplement', *Kinematograph Weekly*, 2 October 1947, p. iv.
26 As quoted in David Fisher, 'The British Film Import Duty 1947–48', Terra Media. Available at: <https://www.terramedia.co.uk/reference/law/british_film_import_duty.htm> (accessed 20 December 2022).
27 Mass Observation, *Meet Yourself on Sunday*, with drawings by Ronald Searle (London: The Naldrett Press, 1949), pp. 15, 57.
28 Labour MP for Cardiff West during the Second Reading of the Sunday Observance Bill, *HC Deb*, 30 January 1953, vol. 510, cc. 1401.
29 Mass Observation, *Meet Yourself*, p. 43.
30 For advocates of the Christian Sunday, see, for example, *Joy and Light: The Lord's Day Magazine* published by the Lord's Day Observance Society. Debates on the lifting of legal restrictions were held in the House of Lords and the House of Commons throughout the 1950s.
31 Collier, *A Film in the Making*, p. 68.
32 François Truffaut, *Hitchcock* (London: Paladin, 1978), p. 140.
33 In fact, the location shots of Coronet Grove were filmed in Camden Town, in north London, although they double up convincingly for the look and feel of East End residential streets.
34 Peter Wollen, 'Architecture and Film', in *Paris Hollywood: Writings on Film* (London and New York: Verso, 2002), p. 204.
35 Collier, *A Film in the Making*, p. 65.
36 Ben Highmore, *The Great Indoors: At Home in the Modern British House* (London: Profile Books, 2014), p. 95. The visitor to the 'Modern Homes' exhibition is quoted on p. 88.
37 See also Hester's suicide attempt in Terence Rattigan's brilliant 1952 play *The Deep Blue Sea*. In 1954, the BBC broadcast an adaptation of the play in its *Sunday Night Theatre* (1950–9) strand in which Googie Withers played Hester. She later toured Australia with the play in this role.
38 For a fascinating discussion of the mantelpiece and MO anthropology, see Rachel Hurdley, 'Mass Observation Fireplaces', in *Home, Materiality, Memory and Belonging: Keeping Culture* (Basingstoke: Palgrave, 2013), pp. 51–78 and esp. p. 60.
39 *Spectator*, 12 December 1947; *Graphic*, 28 November 1947; *Daily Worker*, 29 November 1947; D. A. Yerrill,

'The Technique of Realism', *Sight and Sound* vol. 17, no. 65 (Spring 1948), p. 24.
40 Siegfried Kracauer, *Theory of Film: The Redemption of Physical Reality* (New York: Oxford University Press, 1960), p. 304.
41 Dilys Powell, *Sunday Times*, 30 November 1947.
42 Paul Dehn, *Daily Chronicle*, 30 November 1947.
43 These are, of course, themes also explored by David Lean in his 1945 film *Brief Encounter*. For an excellent discussion of *It Always* in this context, alongside *Cage of Gold* (1950) and *Dance Hall* (1950), see Christine Geraghty, *British Cinema in the Fifties: Gender, Genre and the 'New Look'* (London and New York: Routledge, 2000).
44 La Bern, *It Always*, p. 30.
45 Quoted in Brian McFarlane *An Autobiography of British Cinema as Told by the Filmmakers and Actors Who Made It* (London: Methuen, 1997), p. 610. For Withers's biography, see Brian McFarlane, 'Ingénues, Lovers, Wives and Mothers: The 1940s Career Trajectories of Googie Withers and Phyllis Calvert', in Melanie Bell and Melanie Williams (eds), *British Women's Cinema* (London and New York: Routledge, 2010), pp. 62–76, and Brian McFarlane, *Double-Act: The Remarkable Lives and Careers of Googie Withers and John McCallum* (Clayton, Vic.: Monash University Publishing, 2015).
46 For a full discussion of blonde glamour, see Lynda Nead, *British Blonde: Women, Desire and the Image in Post-War Britain* (New Haven, CT, and London: Yale University Press for the Paul Mellon Centre for Studies in British Art, 2025).
47 Pearl Jephcott, *Rising Twenty: Notes on Some Ordinary Girls* (London: Faber and Faber, 1948), p. 62.
48 Charlotte Brunsdon, 'Space in the British Crime Film', in Steve Chibnall and Robert Murphy (eds), *British Crime Cinema* (London and New York: Routledge, 1999), p. 150.
49 Geraghty, *British Cinema*, pp. 89, 88.
50 C. A. Lejeune, *Observer*, 20 November 1947.
51 Robert Murphy coined the term 'spiv cycle' in *Realism and Tinsel: Cinema and Society in Britain 1939–48* (London and New York: Routledge, 1989). See also Robert Murphy, 'Riff-Raff: British Cinema and the Underworld', in Charles Barr (ed.), *All Our Yesterdays: 90 Years of British Cinema* (London: BFI, 1986), pp. 286–305, and Peter Wollen, 'Riff-Raff Realism', in *Paris Hollywood*, pp. 183–96.
52 The film's marketing emphasised this identification, suggesting that cinemas should dress their commissionaire as a spiv. *It Always Rains on Sunday*, Pressbook, medium, PBM 33754, Pressbooks Collection, BFI National Archive. For a general discussion of men in British cinema in this period, see Andrew Spicer, *Typical Men: The Representation of Masculinity in Popular British Cinema* (London and New York: I. B. Tauris, 2001).
53 The Flash Harry character played by George Cole in *The Belles of St. Trinian's* (1954) is the epitome of the comic spiv.
54 For an excellent discussion of the spiv, see Mark Roodhouse, '"No Basic, More Spivs": Public Endorsement', in *Black Market Britain: 1939–1955* (Oxford: Oxford University Press, 2013), pp. 225–52.

55 Bill Naughton, 'The Spiv', in Charles Madge (ed.), *Pilot Papers: Social Essays and Documents* no. 1 (London: The Pilot Press, 1945), pp. 99–108.
56 Bill Naughton, *News Chronicle*, 13 September 1945.
57 Alexandros Papadopoulos, 'A Violent Archaeology of Dreams: The Aesthetics of Crime in Austerity Britain, c. 1944–1950', PhD thesis, University of Manchester (2011), p. 8.
58 Peter Forbes, 'Spivs', *People*, 3 August 1947.
59 Collier, *A Film in the Making*, p. 63.
60 Ethel Mannin, 'The Trouble with Young People', *People*, 16 March 1947.
61 Naughton, 'The Spiv', p. 105.
62 Collier, *A Film in the Making*, p. 20.
63 For discussion of the links between austerity and antisemitism in Britain in this period, see Tony Kushner, 'Anti-semitism and Austerity: The August 1947 Riots in Britain', in Panikos Panayi (ed.), *Racial Violence in Britain 1840–1950* (Leicester: Leicester University Press, 1993), pp. 149–68, and Daniel Trilling, 'Britain's Last Anti-Jewish Riots', *New Statesman*, 23 May 2012; updated 22 December 2012. Available at: <https://www.newstatesman.com/long-reads/2012/05/britains-last-anti-Jewish-riots> (accessed 6 May 2024).
64 Letter from Rev. L. Shaposnick to Michael Balcon, 3 December 1947, MEB G/71 1/2, Special Collections, BFI National Archive.
65 *Daily Express*, 28 November 1947.
66 The IZL was a Zionist paramilitary organisation that operated in Mandatory Palestine between 1931 and 1948, carrying out acts of extreme violence against the British, whom they regarded as an occupying force; they were also violently anti-Arab. Accounts vary regarding the number and location of the device(s); some say they were buried in the ground between the bodies, others that the bodies themselves were booby-trapped.

Credits

It Always Rains on Sunday
UK
1947

Directed by
Robert Hamer
Produced by
Michael Balcon
Production Company
Ealing Studios

J. Arthur Rank presents
An Ealing Studios Production
Released through General Film Distributors Ltd

Screenplay by
Angus MacPhail
Robert Hamer
Henry Cornelius
From the novel by
Arthur La Bern
Associate Producer
Henry Cornelius
Director of Photography
Douglas Slocombe
Editor
Michael Truman
Production Supervisor
Hal Mason
Art Director
Duncan Sutherland
Sound Supervisor
Stephen Dalby
Recordist
George Diamond
Camera Operator
Jeff Seaholme
Unit Manager
Slim Hand
Make-up
Ernest Taylor
Hairstyles
Doreen Hard
Special Effects
C. Richardson
R. Dendy
Wardrobe Supervisor
Anthony Mendleson
Miss Googie Withers' Frocks Designed by
Horrockses Fashions Ltd
Incidental Music Composed by
Georges Auric
Music Played by
The Philharmonia Orchestra
Conducted by
Ernest Irving
Song 'Theme Without Words' Composed by
Mischa Spoliansky
Dance Music Arranged and Played by
Stanley Black
W. Pogson

CAST
Googie Withers
Rose Sandigate
Edward Chapman
George Sandigate
Susan Shaw
Vi Sandigate
Patricia Plunkett
Doris Sandigate
David Lines
Alfie Sandigate
Sydney Tafler
Morry Hyams
Betty Ann Davies
Sadie Hyams, Morry's wife
John Slater
Lou Hyams, Morry's brother
Jane Hylton
Bessie, Morry's sister
Meier Tzelniker
Solly, Morry's father
John McCallum
Tommy Swann
Jimmy Hanley
Whitey
John Carol
Freddie
Alfie Bass
Dicey
Jack Warner
Det Sgt Fothergill
Frederick Piper
Det Sgt Leech
Michael Howard
Slopey Collins
Hermione Baddeley
Mrs Spry
Nigel Stock
Ted Edwards
John Salew
Caleb Neesley
Gladys Henson
Mrs Neesley
Edie Martin
Mrs Watson
Betty Baskcomb
barmaid of The Two Compasses

Gilbert Davis
governor of The
Two Compasses
Al Millen
Bill Hawkins
Vida Hope
Mrs Wallis
Arthur Hambling
yardmaster
Grace Arnold
Ted's landlady
John Vere
Rev. Black
Patrick Jones
Chuck Evans
Joe E. Carr
Joe
Fred Griffiths
Sam
Francis O'Rawe
Bertie Potts
David Knox
newspaper boy

Production Details
35mm
1.33:1
Black and white
Mono
Running time:
92 minutes

Release Details
UK theatrical release
(limited) in 1947 and
(general) 1948 by General
Film Distributors
US theatrical release
on 12 February 1949 by
Eagle-Lion Films